# METAVERSE

A Beginner's Guide to Investing and Making Passive Income in Virtual Lands, Nft (Crypto Art), Blockchain and Cryptocurrency + 10 Best Defi Projects and Strategies to Maximize Your Profits.

# Contents

# Introduction

Metaverse is an open-world virtual reality platform accessed through The Metaverse Browser. They are both a part of the same system, and they are working together to develop it by making more applications and adventures available and creating more content. The world of metaverse has diverse games, movies, shows, podcasts, educational facilities, and other types of multimedia entertainment. The Metaverse team makes sure that their users are getting the best of experience each day, hence find new ways to improve the performance of their platform.

Metaverse combines multiple elements of technology: virtual reality, augmented reality, and video. Virtual reality is most known for its immersive, three-dimensional, and graphic experience. Augmented reality is an extension of virtual reality, and it is made up of different layers. It contains maps, pictures, videos, alerts, texts, and other graphical data that can be viewed through a computer or mobile device.

The Metaverse platform was officially launched in 2017, and the basic idea was to convert digital assets from the blockchain into a non-fungible token. The non-fungible token can have many possibilities other than the platform's users. It is also called VR (virtual reality) assets or MVSO (Metaverse Virtual Smart Object). Augmented reality is the interaction with the real world, boosted by the computer's interface. Video created using live streams or video recorded on a smartphone is considered an application.

Metaverse Browser also plays a crucial role in all of this. The browser is the only way to access their virtual world through virtual reality devices like Oculus Rift and HTC Vive or Google Cardboard if it is not available to you yet. The Metaverse Application consists of three main concepts. The first is technological and social, the virtual world called "Metaverse," which has infinite possibilities and unlimited opportunities, as it is multi-dimensional. Another con is being able to experience the world from many different points of view so that you can see everything from every conceivable angle. The third concept will be to be your boss and create your universe.

It is an open-source project developing its concepts, ideas, and projects. The Metaverse team is composed of real people with passions, and they are passionate about making The Metaverse come to life.

The Metaverse is a world where you can be anyone and do anything. It's an entirely open-ended virtual world, which means that you are free to do whatever you want because there aren't any restrictions. Making your universe can be done as long as it doesn't violate any laws or infringe on the rights of others. There are still things to come into play when The Metaverse is completed, but there is already a lot that can be done. Metaverse is an exciting concept, and it's an exciting way of creating virtual reality. You can be whoever you want to be and do whatever you want to do, as long as it doesn't violate the laws of the country that you're currently in. Everyone will find their niche in this universe, and the possibilities are endless.

The m is a whole new frontier that can change the way people think about entertainment in general. It can provide a whole new realm of possibilities that have not yet been explored. This virtual reality platform brings about the idea that no matter what you're interested in for entertainment, you will be able to find it on here. Other people looking for similar things will see you on metaverse well. This virtual world is an exciting concept, and its potentials are endless. It has limitless possibilities, and there is absolutely no limit to what you can do within it. As long as it doesn't violate any laws, anything goes in this world, and unlimited opportunities exist.

We shall look into The Metaverse concept and its features in more detail. It will give you a better idea of what it is, who is below you can get involved in the future.

Metaverse is a virtual wan entirely open-ended virtual world with no limits at all within The Metaverse. You can create whatever you want, be whoever you want to be, and do whatever you wish within this world. The possibilities are endless within this universe, and it will most likely change the way people think about entertainment forever.

Metaverse is a platform that gives users the freedom to create their own unique virtual reality experiences. Allowing developers to use The Metaverse SDK to add interactive easily, 3D content into their applications Incorporating 3D content into their apps offers up a whole new universe of possibilities for virtual reality gaming in the future. Metaverse allows users to experience the most immersive and fluid virtual reality gaming ever without calling upon any other companies for assistance.

Metaverse comes a long way from where it started, and it is expected to get even better. Metaverse is a technology platform that different applications can be created off of by various developers. With the help of this technology, there are endless possibilities for what you can do with metaverse and limitless opportunities to find entertainment within it.

Metaverse is also a social platform that allows users to connect with like-minded people across the globe. It has no restrictions on how many individuals you can chat to or interact with; the possibilities are endless.

Metaverse is an open-source project developing its concepts, ideas, and projects. The Metaverse team is composed of real people with passions, and they are passionate about making The Metaverse come to life. The Metaverse is a world where you can be anyone and do anything, and it's an entirely open-ended virtual world, which means that you are free to do whatever you want because there aren't any restrictions.

This book discusses how The Metaverse operates and how it will change the world. It discusses all of the aspects of The Metaverse, and it explains why this platform is going to change everything. It also tells what it is, how to use it, and how to make your own virtual reality experiences to get the most out of this technology. The book is currently in its first edition and is constantly updated to keep up with changes within Virtual Reality and changes within The Metaverse itself.

The Metaverse is an open-source project developing its concepts, ideas, and projects. The Metaverse team is composed of real people with passions, and they are passionate about making The Metaverse come to life.

# Chapter 1 The concept of Metaverse

## So, what is this concept?

 The Metaverse is a term for the internet and virtual reality. By combining these two concepts, we create an online world in which users can enter, interact with other users and digital entities, produce and share content on that world, and purchase digital goods/services within it. Users can perceive their surroundings in virtual reality or interact with computer-generated imagery (CGI).

Metaverse is often called the "Metaverse Builder." It was created and founded by a group of friends who graduated from Stanford University, who realized the potential behind this exciting new platform. After building up a solid foundation at Stanford, they decided to start their own company and product – which became metaverse.

Metaverses include:

- Virtual worlds and virtual world-like platforms.

- Augmented reality and AR applications.

- Artificial intelligence (AI).

- Robotics.

- Other emerging technologies.

Metaverse is built on top of blockchain technology. Metaverse allows users to create their unique digital universes by defining their own rules and laws. These rules are entirely voluntary as no one can force you to abide by them or be part of The Metaverse mean anyone or any

organization does not control the network nation; you set the only rules for joining Metaverse. Anyone can become a developer for The Metaverse environment if they feel that they have the skills to create something in this space with no specific boundaries or restrictions. The community sets the limit, and you can choose what you want to make; the possibilities are endless.

The Metaverse ecosystem consists of five main components: Virtual reality, digital assets, cryptocurrency, advertising, and blockchain or cryptocurrency. The virtual world allows users to build anything they can imagine. Therefore, any creativity is encouraged and necessary for this technology to benefit all users.

When creating your virtual universe, you can define a set of rules – or laws – which control how others voluntarily interact with your universe. one can be a creator or a consumer within The Metaverse. So much so that there is no charge to create or join metaverse. All virtual universes within the network are supported by blockchain technology, which metaverse uses to run its currency (MTV). The currency is called "metaverse," generally referred to as The Metaverse Unit of Determination. There are also other currencies used within metaverse, including ETH and BTC.

Metaverses can be seen as a new type of global internet with its currency, blockchain-based rules and laws, digital assets, digital identities, crypto-money transactions, and an online world that allows users to play roles they create themselves.

## Metaverse

A metaverse is a network of fictional universes within our galaxy that allows for immersive interactions. Virtual spaces, or virtual worlds, can enter into contact with each other, and these new ideas in the market demand a more holistic perspective of the power of virtual reality.

It is a world that transcends any constraint. It is a world whose existence has been implied for hundreds of years, but it has been impossible to develop recently.

The Metaverse idea had been around as long ago as the 1980s, with the introduction of virtual reality (VR) technology. However, there were discussions about a metaverse even before virtual reality was born.

This idea was not just limited to science fiction authors and others in the early days of the internet. In 1994, a then-missing piece of virtual reality was found by two MIT students. Through an experiment, they created an ethernet network where everything could be accessed from anywhere, even from a desktop computer in your basement.

The two students' invention was received with little fanfare, despite being one of the first attempts to create a global communication system.

Since then, however, several companies have emerged as innovators in this emerging technology; one company says they are at "the forefront of research into Metaverse technologies.

To most people, the idea of entering a virtual world and interacting with other people there seems like some science-fiction fantasyland. Still, it has become a reality known as The Metaverse for many. With so many subcultures that thrive within this larger culture, what is possible here in terms of creativity? No one knows definitively, but it is clear that this new area has much potential.

# History of The Metaverse

The Metaverse, we will soon find out, is a term for a concept that had once been called The Exotropia and was later dubbed cyberspace. The Metaverse concept can be dated back to Jaron Lanier's book of the same name, published in 1991.

Neal Stephenson expanded on this concept a few years later in his 1994 novel Snow Crash. In 1994, VPL Research, which specialized in visual reality products and services, released the Data Glove. After the release of this product, Jaron Lanier found VPL Research.

The possibilities for virtual reality and virtual worlds were immense at this time. It was not long until Jaron Lanier, Neal Stephenson, and VPL Research had all independently begun working on the new idea. In 1995, VPL Research developed its network-ready Data Glove product. In the same year, they created The Virtual Fixtures system, which could create real objects within virtual worlds using 3D graphics.

In the same year, Stephenson published a novel involving virtual reality and cyberspace entitled Snow Crash. This novel helped to popularize the idea of a metaverse and be an inspiration for the creation of Second Life. On October 22nd, 1994, Jaron Lanier founded VPL Research, and he began working on his invention, The EyePhone. VPL was focused on creating a visual operating system that would allow users to view and manipulate 3D images in real-time.

In 1995, Jaron Lanier co-founded VPL Research with a few others and began working on his ideas for The Metaverse. Lanier started developing an early version of the VR system at this time. He later called this product "The Grid" in Snow Crash.

After Microsoft had acquired him, Jaron Lanier founded the company behind The Grid - Virtually Real, Inc. He also became involved in IMAX Corporation. Many other companies have been developing their virtual world technologies over the years. In 1999, the company Linden Lab was founded to create a more advanced version of The Grid. Linden Lab became very popular and is currently one of the most well-known and prestigious companies in its field.

# The potential of The Metaverse;

- A new way of doing business; and a new way of interacting with each other are elements that should be considered when creating The Metaverse and its technologies.
- Metaverses, or networks of online worlds, have become increasingly popular as the internet develops. There has been much speculation about what constitutes a metaverse, but very few people have virtual worlds centralized in this way.

- The Metaverse could make for an exciting way for people to meet, socialize and interact with other users. In this way, The Metaverse could function as a virtual community
- Having such a large amount of people (and their avatars) in one area enables new forms of communication and interaction that would not have been possible before. For instance, if everyone in the world were to share an avatar, it would be possible for those people to communicate directly and those avatars to communicate with each other. Furthermore, it would be much easier for people to interact through their avatars than now in real life, allowing even more interaction between users using these online worlds.
- As users share immersive content and interact with each other through their avatars, they will also develop relationships and bonds built over time. This will also c community, as these users will eventually have many things in common.
- Metaverses have been created for a particular purpose and designed to achieve this goal. The Metaverse helps people live out their online lives that would not be possible if this technology were unavailable.
Common characteristics of metaverse include:
1. Virtual worlds that are interconnected and accessible from any computer or device through the use of computer-generated graphics (CGI), such as virtual reality technology
2. They tend to be persistent; they do not usually end after a single interaction
3. An individual or group of people usually creates the worlds in The Metaverse; they are not based on reality, and they have their own set of rules
4. These worlds are often accessible through personal computers or other devices without requiring users to enter a designated space, such as a separate room. For this to be possible, virtual reality technology such as virtual reality goggles are required
5. Real-time communication is required for people from different worlds to communicate at times. This may require additional hardware such as microphones and headphones, in addition to virtual reality hardware.
6. can use any available space for this type of content. Due to the nature of The Metaverse, it is possible to create spaces that are simply visual representations.

## Advantages of The Metaverse

- Many people have speculated about the benefits of The Metaverse. People may, for example, interact with more people, undertake more actions, and complete more tasks. Potential consumers find the prospect of being in a room with a bunch of other consumers is enticing. Such an experience would be impossible to provide without virtual reality hardware that allows users to choose from a variety of interfaces.
- It will be possible for information from one world to spread rapidly into other worlds. This means that it would be much easier for people to learn about news from other planets or even meet new friends

- It will be possible for several users to interact with each other at once in a shared environment. It would be beneficial in a variety of situations, such as when users are required to take a test or engage in a conversation.
- People may improve their performance in school or work more efficiently.
- It will be possible for people to have a virtual job that they can learn and practice at home so that it does not interfere with their regular life.
- People may simulate sports through technology such as virtual reality goggles, which could help people train and perform better when playing competitive sports.

## Disadvantages of The Metaverse

- People from other worlds may not accept new cultures that are created in The Metaverse. Such cultures could include anything from different languages to different religions and can be created by either a professional or an amateur.
- It is possible that users will feel like they are wasting their time when they have no real purpose in the world, which could make them feel somewhat worthless.
- Some users may feel as though they are not learning anything when they use virtual worlds if they don't interact with real people.
- Users may feel as though they are unable to get what they want out of The Metaverse because not everything is possible to achieve without advanced technology
Metaverse community is based on a core activity of virtual community – online communication for online people. Metaverses can work as a social network, with the primary goal of creating a virtual world that feels real.
With this goal comes choices about the communities' laws and values, which will be used to create the rules and customs of The Metaverse community.

# Chapter 2 Virtual Reality

## What Is Virtual Reality?

Virtual reality is an immersive computer-generated 3D environment that can be explored and interacted with. The user can navigate the virtual world using a headset, typically equipped with two screens for each eye; these screens send separate images to each eye, creating a sense of depth.

How to collect data for the 3D environment.

A positional tracking system uses a combination of video cameras and sensors to track the user's head movements. In addition to head tracking and display output, VR systems use inputs such as joysticks, gamepads, and keyboards or voice recognition systems for control. The computer processes the user's movements in real-time to update the 3D visuals to appear lifelike and obey the laws of physics within the virtual space.

Computer technology creates virtual worlds that users can interact with using head-mounted displays or a controller on their physical body. VR is not limited to video games; it could be as simple as an online shopping experience or even something like watching Netflix. Virtual reality can use unique human-computer interaction, allowing for more realistic experiences and satisfying diversions. It provides many benefits to the economy, employment opportunities, and health care systems worldwide.

It's no wonder why this technology has caught on so quickly, and people are clamoring for it now more than ever.

## Types of virtual reality

There are different types of virtual reality.

- 3D Computer-generated environments in which users can interact with the environment with their controllers. This could be a simple game experience or a complete 3D walk-through of science fiction or fantasy worlds. The technology used to produce these environments is VRML (Virtual Reality Modeling Language), and it allows designers to create large, complex environments that can easily navigate using head-tracked displays. The main limitations of this form of VR are that the experience is single-user, the user must have a reasonably powerful PC to run, and it requires special software for each PC to run.

- Physical environments, or full-body experiences, where users enter the virtual environment. This form of VR is usually only accessible to those with special equipment for the process (such as a suit or helmet) designed for the experience. This is usually a minimal experience and has less flexibility for gameplay because it can only be navigated through a limited number of movement options with the body.
- Augmented reality combines physical and virtual reality so that users can see their natural environment overlaid on top of their virtual world. This would be similar to the Pokémon Go game, where players can use their smartphones to find Pokémon in the real world. - The concept of augmented reality technologies has existed for decades, with some of the first being "Magic Glasses," which were invented in 1891 by Louis J. Cozia, who wore a pair of mirrored glasses to let users look around a natural environment and see it as if it were a computer game. The first
known researcher to develop this technology was Jaron Lanier, who created "Augmented Conversations" before it became popular with the development of smartphones in 2007.
- Mixed reality. VR, augmented reality, and physical reality all come together so that users can see them in addition to their virtual or natural environment. This is different from AR because it's not only the user's surroundings — it's the user themselves and their environment all combined. Imagine yourself as a digital 3D avatar, and your body is part of the virtual world. It's like Groundhog Day, but the digital avatar is you.

## How Does Virtual Reality Work?

Virtual reality works using a combo of sensors, software, and hardware connected to deliver a multisensory experience. It can be done using a computer, monitors, and special software to process the user's movements within a 3D environment. The concept of VR began with a need for accurate human-machine interfaces. The first documented account of this was in the 1800s when Paul Julius Gottfried Ludwig von Bertalanffy, an Austrian scientist, proposed the idea of "synthetic panoramas" or synthetic environments created through a combination of sensory inputs like sight and sound.

Today, users interact with virtual worlds through virtual reality headsets known as head-mounted displays or HMDs. Just like a pair of binoculars and a filter that allows only specific wavelengths to be seen by each eye. However, VR is used as a full-screen interpupillary distance (IPD)
adjustment system that will enable you to see close objects at the same ideal distance between your eyes in real life.

Typically, most Virtual Reality headsets work with a PC and require specialized software to work. For example, Oculus Rift's headset works with the Oculus rift program on PC, and its Touch controllers work with the hand tracking software on PC and mobile devices. Vive and the HTC Vive work with SteamVR, a software platform compatible with PCs and gaming consoles.

Virtual reality headsets feature two cameras mounted behind the lenses for stereo vision. The cameras use image processing and record the user's surroundings in 3D, allowing them to see through their virtual environments.

Types of sensors that are used in VR headsets:

Rotational digital accelerometers, which detect movement (e.g., turning your head or turning your body)

External optical motion sensors .

Position sensors that detect how far you can extend your hand.

Ambient light sensors to measure brightness falling on the eyes.

## Types of Virtual Reality Devices

1- Non-immersive Virtual Reality headsets - The most popular VR headsets are non-immersive. They use a smartphone as the display and run VR apps on it. They are easy to wear and do not require any connections to a PC. The problem with these is that because they are

non-immersive, it is hard to track the user's movement, making the experience tiresome after a few minutes of use.

2- Semi-Immersive Virtual Reality headsets are also known as stand-alone virtual reality (VR) headsets. They can be used with or without mobile devices, although they require a high level of hardware and processing performance. These are used primarily for gaming purposes.

3- Fully Immersive Virtual Reality headsets - These VR headsets have all of the required components for virtual reality to work. They can be connected to a PC and are usually used in industrial and academic environments.

4- Augmented Reality headset is different from virtual reality because it adds information about the user's surroundings and displays a virtual environment. The most famous example is Google Glass, which uses optical head-mounted displays (OHMDs). While wearing them, users can see their surroundings and additional digital d overlaid on their natural environments via small screens inside their glasses.

5- Mixed Reality headset - This is interaction with a VR or AR environment, along with the real natural environment. Mixed reality headsets allow the user to interact in both environments.

6- Virtual - Augmented Reality (VAR) – Interaction with a virtual or augmented reality environment and their natural environment. Both settings are overlaid on top of each other.

## How do you make a virtual reality experience?

There are different approaches that different companies have taken. For example, the Samsung Gear VR has a touchpad and rotational sensors built right into the headset, used in conjunction with the Galaxy smartphones to sense the user's hand movement. Google Cardboard is similar in that it does not include additional equipment besides a smartphone to work. Other types of VR headsets include Vuze, Vuzix Wrap 1200, LG 360 CAM-VR, Oculus Rift DK1 and DK2s, HTC Vive, Valve Roomscale VR and Sony PlayStation VR.

## Virtual Reality Trends and Future Directions

Virtual reality technology is still being developed, but it has come a long way from its initial beginnings around 90 years ago. Things such as digital content, application support, user interfaces, and computer vision have improved accessibility and usefulness for people in most fields of work. With this development, virtual reality is set to become a massive part of the future, and significant factors will influence the evolution in this field. A lot that needs to be done on virtual reality, but some of its consequences can have positive and negative outcomes in today's world. Virtual reality technology could help or hinder people in different areas such as medicine, education, hospitality, and entertainment. For example, virtual reality games could bring joy and relaxation to people who suffer from anxiety disorders, so they can experience playing with other people rather than being alone.

# Chapter 3 Augmented Reality.

What is augmented reality?

Augmented Reality is the projection of digital information (text, graphics, sound, etc.) on the environment in real-time to augment an existing reality. Augmented Reality is one of the more recent emerging technologies. Augmented Reality is not simply a case of projecting information onto a computer screen. Augmented Reality presents a natural environment where the virtual object co-exists in real-time with the natural world. We can refer to this as extended reality.

Augmented reality is a multi-media application that uses your vision, sound, and motion-sensing by using visible electronic markers placed over or on top of objects in the real world.

Augmented Reality is a technology that blends natural and digital worlds to create new environments and visualizations where physical objects and digital information are combined in real-time.

Augmented comes from the word raise, which means to increase or intensify. Augmentation is a modification that involves using additional or supplementary components. If this were done with a car, it would mean adding something (like a spoiler) to increase speed or performance capability; in this case, the natural world is augmented by virtual information, which enhances its performance capability beyond what it could do on its own. The term Virtual is often used to refer to the computer-simulated

Augmented reality is a new form of information technology that can enhance work, play, and learning. A process called "augmenting" is performed in the real world, and the augmented world contains a digital representation of the physical world.

Augmented reality (AR) or AR tech is a technology that brings computer-generated images and virtual objects into proximity to the user's physical environment via head-mounted displays (HMDs). The HMD provides spatial and temporal cues that combine with real-world data such as GPS location, motion sensors, and computer vision to provide users with overlays in the real world.

A World that exists on a monitor or printed page. In the context of Augmented Reality, the term virtual refers to digital information generated using a computing device. However, this digital information does not exist physically but is merely stored on a memory chip. The term Virtual can therefore be regarded as synonymous with Digital information.

There are various types of augmented objects: vision increased objects (virtual video or video images), sound increased objects (audio content), and motion-sensing raised things (motion sensor data). Augmented Reality is the vision of a person wearing a computer or containing a tiny camera that will show virtual objects superimposed on images captured by the cameras. Therefore, it is not a photography, but the ability to see different information through your camera's lens.

Types of Augmented Reality

There are different types of augmentation:

1) VR, Virtual Reality - A virtual or imaginary world entirely constructed by software, often experienced via headsets and other input devices.

2) AR, Augmented Reality - In this model of augmented reality, the view of the natural world is enhanced by computer-generated information in real-time. This can take the shape of supplementary information or visuals (for example, historical events or structures), sounds (music or commentary), or physical sensations (heat or wind).

3) Mixed Reality -The term mixed reality has appeared recently to describe cases where a blend between AR and VR is used. Mixed reality consists of a combination of the enhanced "real" environment with computer-generated elements. Mixed reality takes place not solely in the physical or virtual worlds but is a mix between those worlds.

4) OAR, Object-aware Augmentations (OARs), such as Linking 3D graphics to live television video. Mixed Reality takes place at the same time and place as another reality. The real world can be augmented by computer-generated elements, vice versa, or both.

5) PLAR, Post-Linking Augmented Reality - In this model of augmented reality, the real world is augmented by computer-generated information after a camera has taken the initial picture. This can occur due to being linked to other images on the internet. Alternatively, it might be based on Google Maps data from a mobile phone, which is then used to augment an image.

6) Hiper-Augmented Reality - In this augmented reality model, the real world is augmented by computer-generated information before the camera takes the initial picture.
This usually involves using a small projector to project information onto a surface or object in the real world.

7) Enhanced Reality - A particular type of augmented reality where the Augmented Reality is projected onto an entire surface.

8) Mixed Reality - It is a term for digital information created by augmentation in the real world.

9) Sensor-based Augmented Reality - In this augmented reality model, digital information is created from physical interactions with the environment (for example, light sensors).

There are three types of augmented objects: vision increased objects (virtual video or video images), sound increased objects (audio content), and motion-sensing raised things (motion sensor data). Augmented Reality is often combined with Virtual Reality to create a mixed reality.

Applications of Augmented Reality

Daily, we use our senses of vision, hearing, and touch to engage with the natural environment. Augmented Reality technology enables us to interact with the real world. Still, in addition to sense data provided by those senses, it gives us supplementary visual information and sound information. Such augmentations can occur in several ways: video images or graphics can be overlaid on top of objects, audio messages can be played through a device when a particular object is sensed or felt by a person, or even tactile sensations can be transmitted when a person touches an object.

Such information augmentation forms an integral part of augmented reality, which otherwise refers to a real wholly or partly view of a physical, real world situation with computer-generated sensory input such as sound, video, graphics, or GPS data. This sensory information is then combined with the user's normal perception of the physical realm.

In the 3D space surrounding us, we can experience the sensation of depth and distance between objects. We make these judgments based on our visual perception and previous experiences. Augmented Reality technology enables us to expand existing knowledge by placing virtual objects into the real world and interacting with them naturally.

Google Glass is a recent innovation in this area. This head-mounted wearable computer overlays reality using a small screen above your right eye. This screen shows emails, maps, and directions and can even be used for video chats.

Today's modern smartphones are also widely used for augmented reality applications. For instance, many use Google's mobile map app for real-time navigation. Old roads and buildings are overlaid onto your reality to make the directions clearer, appearing as you travel along a particular route.

Another example is Yelp, a user-generated content app that allows users to view reviews of restaurants, hotels, or businesses in their local area. Users can interact with this data by viewing the information through their mobile camera, augmenting their experience.

There are also AR apps used solely for entertainment purposes. For example, the popular game Ingress uses augmented reality to turn neighborhoods into battlefields between two factions of players.

When AR is referred to as an enhancement of reality, it sometimes means that virtual information is added to change the way we perceive the object.

1. Military training for soldiers. It helps to make their training more realistic, and it gives them a great deal of valuable feedback without them ever having to step onto a battlefield. In one example from a US Army research project, soldiers used an AR helmet to shoot at avatars that appeared as other soldiers. The helmets showed how well they were shooting, and when they hit the targets, it was pretty rewarding for them.

2) AR, Augmented Reality. Augmented reality is being used to show data on top of an image of an object. For example, a user can point their cell phone camera at a product and receive information about that product via AR.

3) Virtual Reality. Virtual Reality has been used in several different ways, as one might expect. One way it is used in a real-world situation to become more familiar with it. For example, pilots use virtual reality to train for landing planes in difficult weather conditions so that if they ever encounter those conditions in real life, they will be prepared for them.

4) MR, Mixed Reality. Mixed Reality is when different types of information are mixed. For example, people can walk around a virtual world and see real-time data simultaneously, which might show how a product works or how to use it.

5) PLAR, Post-Linking Augmented Reality - In this model of augmented reality, the real world is augmented by computer-generated information after a camera has taken the initial picture. This can occur due to being linked to other images on the internet. Alternatively, it might be based on Google Maps data from a mobile phone, which is then used to augment an image.

Extended Reality (XR)

XR is an exciting new discipline in computer graphics combined with reality. XR uses advanced visual processing techniques to create physical interfaces with natural objects. This means that XR uses a particular virtual reality display combined with active sensors and computation to create an interface that includes both virtual and natural elements. It aims to achieve a natural and intuitive way to interact with real and virtual objects. This results in a mixed reality, where the real and virtual worlds are combined. The most critical XR technologies use an HMD or headset that allows interaction with the environment. In some cases, the use of an HMD isn't required, but it's possible to control the interfaces using a keyboard, mouse, or other input devices.

The future of Extended Reality

The future of XR is very interesting and exciting. A lot of work can be done in this area, but it will continue to grow from there. One thing leads to another, and the future looks bright.

The XR is not something we need to create; it's already there, and it's already a part of our world, and we need to realize that it exists.

The XR (extended reality) is an art form that aims to make us feel more connected to other people, our environment, and the world around us. It will become more accessible for people to move through their everyday life being more socially connected with the other people in their field of view, using only voice or gesture recognition and natural movements to communicate.

People spend lots of time each day on social media, and you can feel that it's becoming an addiction. We can't hang out with people who we want to meet just because we can't reach them to invite them for dinner. Leading to the current norm where online communication is the most common way to communicate with the people around us and those with whom we share interests and passions.

At the same time, many people are interested in building bridges between real life and virtual reality.

The greatest way to do this is to enhance real-life enjoyment by providing engaging experiences that go beyond technology. The goal of the XR is to make it possible and easy for people to share their experiences with other people in the real world. The idea here is to allow people in the real world to experience something happening in another location by trying it themselves. This can be done by creating a virtual reality of another person (like we have here) and allowing a person using a headset to experience the scene from another perspective (the one from the street or in something else).

# Chapter 4 Role of NFTs

## The role of NFT in The Metaverse

They are the engine that drives our decentralized economy and improves many of the current problems plaguing blockchains, such as scalability, privacy, and security.

To ensure the long-term health of NFTs in The Metaverse, all developers need to have a basic understanding of how NFTs work before developing any smart contracts themselves. NFTs cannot be exchanged or counterfeited.

Fully tokenized assets in the digital world are known as Non-Fungible Tokens. The concept was developed to allow for digital assets that are unique and can't be duplicated. The idea is that NFTs could be used for almost everything from property, artwork, and services, such as artwork on a blockchain platform or services like property title registration. They can also act as proof of ownership of physical items such as a car or painting.

1. Tokenization of Assets
- The main reason for NFTs is the tokenization of assets, whether they be scarce digital goods or physical assets tied to a digital ID.

NFTs enable full ownership by allowing the owner of the digital assets to be identified. Currently, ownership can only be verified if a third party verifies their identity or through a trust-based system such as escrow.

2. Ownership
- Ownership is how an asset is controlled by someone. With the introduction of NFTs, it will become possible to have full control over your valued asset without any middleman or trust-based system being involved, which will make blockchain more accessible to the average person.

3. Real-estate
- If a physical object can be tokenized, then it will be possible to buy property on the blockchain, which is already one of the most expensive currencies out there. It is an open question whether there will be demand for such contracts in the future. Still, it is possible that NFTs could drive the real estate market in a similar way as Ethereum and NEO are driving the cryptocurrency market.

4. Voting
- It could be possible for a server to issue tokens representing the voter's vote, allowing individuals to create a new chain without miners and thus protect their chain from attacks.

5. Self-sovereign identities-

Digital identity is one of the bigger problems in the real world, but blockchain technology can solve these problems and give users full control over their identities.

6. Insurance and financial services-

Blockchain has the potential to bring us decentralized insurance and financial services that reduce the risk for all parties involved.

Non-profit and charity sectors- Non-profit organizations and charities have a unique way of raising funds. They encourage funders to contribute to their cause in exchange for rewards or tokens, which will give them full ownership of their reward.

8. Content creators–

Content creators could be rewarded for the production of quality content by creating tokens based on engagement, video views, or likes on social media, which will give them a sustainable income stream.

## Impact of NFTs on The Metaverse

1. NFTs impact The Metaverse through the tokenization of digital assets. The biggest impact of NFTs on The Metaverse is that they allow for the full ownership of digital assets. It will be possible to trade these assets, which we can't do today with traditional currencies.

2. NFTs also create another asset class that is based on the value of the digital assets. As NFTs start to grow in value, it will be possible to trade these NFTs as well.

3. Another way NFTs impact The Metaverse is by creating a new sort of digital asset, Non-Fungible tokens (NFT). Although NFTs are similar to fungible tokens, they are also very different in terms of how they are valued.

4. The biggest impact NFTs will have on our society is related to their ability to tokenize physical objects that can then be recorded on the blockchain and traded freely with no restrictions. This will create a whole
new digital economy and will be disruptive for all kinds of current businesses.

5. NFTs also provide new ways of combating the current problems plaguing blockchain. With scalability and security, blockchain is more than a technology for cryptocurrency. It has been used for other applications such as gold on a blockchain, so it makes sense that we will see NFTs applied to anything from digital art to property titles.

## NFTs and our virtual lives

NFTs will give users full ownership over the digital identities they use to own properties and verify their identity in traditional social media. Users can design their value in The Metaverse and exchange it with other users on the market.

With NFTs, users can also own entire artwork, which gives them full ownership of a part of their digital life. The biggest impact NFTs will have is that they will enable everyone to have full ownership over their digital assets and the values they represent.

NFTs could also increase the amount of trust users can put in other people with their identity. To give an example, it could be possible for a bank to issue tokens representing user's account balances and let them trade this on the market. Users will also be able to verify the identities of trustworthy people without any middlemen. This could create a new safe way for users to interact with each other without worrying about a third party being involved.

People will be able to sell digital items on the blockchain. For example, if you are a crypto enthusiast, you might want to sell your digital asset for real-world money instead of just keeping it for the future. The creation of a digital identity is becoming more free and easier with NFTs. If you have created a digital identity and want to join The Metaverse, it is possible to do that with just one click.

NFTs will give people ownership over their identities, and people will start to care about their digital identities because they can own them like any other physical asset. This means that you can use your digital identity on the internet and not just on the blockchain. If you want to know who owns something, The Metaverse could be an appropriate place for that information. You could make money by selling this information like with any other good or service on the market. There could be an increase in trade because NFTs will make it easier for people to exchange different digital assets and receive their value.

In metaverse, we have different types of tokens; each is used for a different purpose. The primary token used on metaverse is the Entropy (ETP). ETP itself does not have any special features; however, other tokens that use ETP as a base platform token derive their own functionality from ETP's capabilities via smart contracts.

# NFTs and our physical lives

- With the ability to tokenize anything, businesses and individuals can use blockchain technology to create NFTs.
- It will be possible for users to have digital identities that are fully
trackable from birth until death. This is expected to have a huge impact on the medical world and insurance industries.
- It will also be possible for people to store their blood samples in a blockchain account where they can track changes in the genome. This will allow them to do genetic research without depending on third parties.

# Chapter 5 Web 3.0

## What is web 3.0?

Web 3.0 is part of the World Wide Web in which the world's data is decentralized and primarily resides on servers. Web 3.0 allows more user control over their data, apps, and storage without a central server.

Web 3.0 was initially described by Tim Berners-Lee in 2001 as an evolution of the current pervasiveness of web applications cooperation with a model for distributed trust and economy, called "Semantic Web."

The next version of the World Wide Web is known as Web 3.0. It is a massive, global, scalable, and ubiquitous information platform that can address a wide variety of information needs.

The next evolution of the World Wide Web is Web 3.0 and its connection with people. The term itself has a vague definition that differs from person to person, but here are some common ideas behind web 3.0:

-It allows for dynamic information sharing and supports personalization

-It blends the virtual and physical worlds seamlessly

-It is created through decentralized collaboration between individuals who share their knowledge freely

It is believed the third generation of the World Wide Web is often described as a place where people control their data and can access trusted. Decentralized applications that enable them to quickly and safely

exchange information with each other without the need to trust intermediaries like Facebook."

Its a term that describes the evolution of the web from Web 2.0. It's a term for many new technologies that people conjecture will transform Apple or Google into something much bigger than they currently are.

Web 3.0 is an approach to web development that focuses on using many tools and services to create, implement, and maintain a website.

Web 3.0 is a "new era of the internet" that will allow ideas and creations to spread without being owned by large companies.

Web 3.0 is not about the technology itself but the new way to interact with digital content and services, mainly through user-generated content, crowdsourcing, user-centric social networks, and a business model based on micropayments rather than advertising.

Web 3.0 is a more semantic version of the current Web. The Semantic Web would allow computers and people to search for data more effectively.

Concept of Web 3.0

It applies the concept of social networking, where the user has a special status. They can be registered in multiple networks have his profile, to which he can add information that is not available on the profile of other users.

Web 3.0 is computer network operating system software that includes a web server embedded in applications. Its main features are its capacity to extend the functionality of existing applications with additional features and provide users with greater control over their data.

Web 3.0 allows more user control over their data, apps, and storage without a central server.

Any single entity does not control the global computer, so it's more secure than centralized systems owned by a few companies or organizations. It also facilitates the development of new decentralized business models that can operate without a central point of failure and are censorship-resistant.

## The emergence of Web 3.0

Web 3.0 has already widely emerged in many forms today, thanks to IoT and Blockchain technologies that have given the go-ahead for the next generation web to flourish. Data marketplaces enable users to monetize their data through a secure platform and gain access to products tailored to their needs and interests. These platforms can process big data using decentralized app development models, which will be deployed on distributed ledgers.

Through the web-based Web 3.0, data can be accessed with businesses across industries in an open, transparent, and secure mode. Moreover, businesses will be able to access the market through valuable services that data vendors provide. It will allow producers of services and products to gain access to consumers' valuable information for their business. Data marketplaces can also be a source of new business opportunities for entrepreneurs.

In addition to launching new products marketed by prominent data vendors, users can drive startups through crowdfunding strategies using their data as a base for their projects. There will be a new platform for fundraising where users can raise funds for their startups on the blockchain. Furthermore, it will also allow non-profit organizations to generate donations from their supporters.

With the help of distributed ledger technologies, features such as scalability, transparency, and high integrity can be achieved. These technological assets have the potential to disrupt current business models.

Blockchain has helped to ensure immutable records of transactions handled using the web. Data marketplaces enable users to monetize their data through a secure platform and gain access to products tailored to their needs and interests. These platforms can process big data using decentralized app development models, which will be deployed on distributed ledgers. Through the web-based Web 3.0, data can be accessed with businesses across industries in an open, transparent, and secure mode. Moreover, businesses will be able to access the market through valuable services that data vendors provide.

## History of Web 3.0

The most significant changes in the Internet are not being developed. They can be traced back to the 90s and 2000s. Internet 2 was formed, which provided a new standard for networking to use the infrastructures of different organizations. Then Web 3.0, which is the next evolution of
the World Wide Web, was released by its inventor Tim Berners-Lee. He projected that the Web's next wave would be utterly different from its current.
Web 2.0 was activated from 2005 to 2010. Web 2.0 is well-known for being a more interactive web and allowing users to connect to their social networks more efficiently than ever before. Companies like Twitter, Facebook, and Google were formed, allowing people to post photos and videos online and share them with anyone worldwide. These are examples of Web 2.0.
Web 3.0 was expected to be fully formed by 2015. Still, some reports on this new system may not fully form until 2020 or even later than that, as new technologies are being incorporated into the internet at a fast rate right now.
This means a lot when compared with current versions of internet technology. His goal is to change how each individual uses their data, which will affect many aspects like cloud storage and applications that have evolved from it. This can be considered as the first generation of cloud services.

## Applications of web 3.0

- The application of Web 3.0 is to make all the services on the internet more accessible, compatible, and easy to use.
-If you want to use the internet, there are many tools you can access through it.

-We can connect to other people through different social networks such as Google+ and Facebook, but some other applications were developed using Web 3.0, for example, Instagram, which allows us to share photos and videos that we take with applications such as Snapchat.

-Everybody has their mobile phone now to communicate with anyone all over the world. Still, they have seen their influence on a bigger scale since Facebook came out in 2006, where users can send messages or leave comments whenever they want and even read their friends' updates.

-One of the most important components of Web 3.0 is that it allows users to send their content freely, as this means that they can store as many documents and pictures on their personal computer and share them with anyone around the world.

-Another aspect that influences web 3.0 is when we use applications such as Uber for ridesharing or Airbnb for renting out our houses so that others can come and stay in our houses or even houses of other people, which is a new approach towards home rentals.

## The Future of Web 3.0

The term "Web 3.0" is a bit confusing because it does not have a concrete definition describing what it is. It is pretty challenging to say where this future web will still go and how this will affect our lives in general, but several trends are emerging, giving us some insight into how Web 3.0 might alter our lifestyles.

First of all, there is the concept of "User Control of Identity" and "Personal Data Privacy." It doesn't look like a big difference today, but we are moving towards a new way of data management where users can manage personal data and use it.

Secondly, there is the concept of a "Sharing Economy."

The emergence of the sharing economy has radically altered the way consumers think about buying and selling goods and services. Nowadays, people buy fewer things because they can use things from other people through different platforms such as Airbnb or Uber. Therefore, this concept can be an essential step in entering Web 3.0. Many other applications are being connected to this new web, but it's hard to predict how it will change our lives in general. If Web 3.0 is formed completely, it will completely change how we see and use the Internet without a doubt.

It's hard to know what the future holds for us, but Web 3.0 will undoubtedly change our interactions with the internet and our online services. We may anticipate a few features from Web 3.0, and most likely, much more when you think about it.

Third, there are two things that we can expect from Web 3.0, and they are "the ability to own your data" and "the ability to harvest your data." From the very beginning, people have been given the possibility to share their own opinions, but now this possibility is extended to sharing our other personal information. For example: if you want to check the
weather forecast in different cities, then with Web 3.0, you will access this information directly from some of your friends because they have already shared it with you.
Even though these two points are great for users and companies, this means that almost all personal data has commercial value.
Web 3.0 is expected to have a more advanced and more prosperous user experience and social interaction. Web 3.0 is the future, but it should also be the present. In other words, we should be seeing Web 3.0 applications appear soon, not just conceptually or in the distant future. And we are already seeing how Web 3.0 could affect our lives and improve it overall with new ideas on how to manage our data, or even see what someone else has shared about us with all our friends connected through different platforms like Skype or Facebook for example.

# Chapter 6 Virtual real estate investing.

## What is Virtual real estate investing?

Virtual real estate investing is a style of real estate investing that involves buying, selling, managing, and renting out properties virtually.

This is a simple step to start real estate investing without cash.

Virtual real estate investing is typically accomplished using fixed-rate notes. Fixed-rate notes are promissory notes used as investments secured by a mortgage on income-producing property. They provide returns on principal investments to the note owner and generate monthly payments to the mortgage lender.

In virtual real estate, the property is not accurate. In other words, it is not physical and cannot be seen or touched. This makes it challenging to meet with your clients face-to-face and rent the property. Therefore, when you show the property, you must always use virtual reality software (such as VirtualReality) to show the property in an easy-to-locate manner. Building trust with a potential renter requires a more personal touch – just like winning over new clients for traditional real estate agents.

## How does virtual real estate investing work?

The process involves the creation of virtual properties that represent digital liens on physical properties and then buying and selling these virtual properties through licensed exchanges like Second Life or World Ventures Platform based on supply and demand principles.

The buying and selling process is similar to any other real estate investing, and the difference is in the method of creating the property. In the real world, properties are sold and bought by investment groups.

But in the world of virtual reality, buying and selling real estate is done by individuals. You acquire your virtual land, which you can then use for building a house, a hotel, an online business, an online shop, or whatever you want. When you lease the property to someone else, it becomes a debt owed to you on the property.

Real estate was the primary focus of early virtual worlds such as Second Life and Entropia Universe. The idea of creating digital real estate was to give users a way to demonstrate their wealth and status in the game world. The idea was that users could purchase land inside a game based on game space to create virtual homes, businesses, and even entire towns that could be sold later if they no longer wanted them or needed additional cash.

The virtual world is already populated with millions of residents - this gives virtual real estate investors an advantage over their counterparts who are limited to buying and selling only 3 – 8 properties in a physical market.

## Getting started in Virtual Real Estate Investing.

You will need to determine the specific real estate market you're interested in.
Many real estate forms can be purchased and sold using fixed-rate notes. Here are some examples:
Property types that sell on a traditional open market include:
• Single-family homes
• Duplexes
• Condominiums
• Manufactured homes

## How to Choose a Real Estate Market.

Choosing a real estate market is a crucial decision that several factors can influence, and it's a decision that will likely significantly impact your bottom line.
Your market choice should be based on your knowledge of the real estate market and the history of the market you are considering. It would be best to be mindful of potential long-term interest rate trends since this significantly impacts the sustainable income you can achieve in your chosen real estate market.
Three main factors influence real estate values: Local supply and demand, national economic trends, and interest rates. These factors will either increase or decrease property values. If an order is high and supply is low, prices can quickly grow. If an order is insufficient and collection is high, prices can quickly decrease.
Suppose you're thinking of investing in or developing properties in a particular real estate market. In that case, you must have a complete understanding of the market, its history, and your ability to make money with that market.

## Making an Investment Decision

Making an Investment Decision is a crucial step in the real estate process.
It's an action that can have significant consequences.
The decision-making process typically consists of a few simple steps:

1. Research your market - research the local property taxes, growth rates, payback periods, and cost of living. Research the commercial market in general. Discover the real estate values in the city where you would like to invest. Compare them against other cities you are considering investing in.

2. Analyze your market - Look at a variety of investment and rental properties you could purchase to see what it cost and how much money they would generate for you using a site like Zillow

3. Compile a list - compile a list of prospective properties based on the research and analysis you conducted in the first step. It can be as simple as Microsoft Word or as complex as an elaborate decision tree.

4. Develop an investment calendar - develop a plan that matches the real estate you are interested in growing with the right property type. You must be aware of your time frame and whether any additional conditions need to be met to accommodate this plan. Depending on your criteria, you may even want to consider investing in different real estate markets at other times during your time frame – for example, at three different intervals between right before and right after retirement.

## Market research

For any business, analyzing the market is critical for any real estate purchase or development project. It is essential when investing in a new market or making a new investment within an existing market.

Market research delivers valuable market insights that help you reduce risks, avoid costly mistakes, and open opportunities for profit. It provides a roadmap to the latest trends in your market that can significantly affect your bottom line.

The best research is focused on answering specific questions about the market, and information gathered from your own experience and others can provide valuable data points. Still, it's essential to verify their accuracy, so they don't lead you down the wrong path. Being armed with reliable information at every step of the process gives you a massive advantage over those who aren't—and it positions you to maximize profits better when new opportunities present themselves.

Market research is critical for every real estate purchase or development project. Doing it well will help you avoid costly mistakes and open doors for new opportunities to profit. It also helps position you to maximize profits when new opportunities present themselves.

To ensure you have a successful investment, many market researchers provide an in-depth analysis of the market and recommend how it may perform in the future. But to gain that insight, you need to do your research.

The purpose of market research is to:
- Gain a clear understanding of potential opportunities and risks
- Evaluate information coming from different sources
- Reduce risks by confirming or modifying your initial decision
- Estimate the return on investment (ROI) for your chosen real estate option

## What are the benefits of Virtual Real Estate Investing?

1. Anonymity - Virtual investing will allow you to invest in real estate without revealing your identity in the online world. If you want to invest in different markets at different times and locations, it can also safeguard personal anonymity

2. Growing with the economy - Virtual real estate investing helps investors grow with the economy, providing a way to capitalize on growth rates when they are high and adapt quickly when the market changes.

3. No travel required – Virtual real estate investing allows investors to invest in various markets globally without having to travel.

4. Diversification - Virtual real estate investing helps diversify your investment portfolio.

5. Faster transactions are much faster than completing transactions on the physical market, providing an advantage over traditional real estate investing models. When you make an offer on a piece of property, it's done in minutes, while conventional methods of buying can take months to close.

## Risks associated with virtual real estate investing

That being said, there are several risks associated with virtual real estate investing.
- For one, you are trusting a virtual person with your funds. There is no physical security for your investment, and it can be much more difficult to recover funds should the relationship end violently.
- You must also be careful when choosing where you work based on your location. Suppose a company is located in an area that is hard hit by riots, c, crime, or another significant event. In that case, it might be impossible to collect any proceeds once the situation has passed.

- Another concern is that because virtual investing involves dealing with multiple individuals simultaneously, there is a high risk of fraud and errors in the process, which could put you at risk of losing money or worse if there is a problem with networking or communication during a transaction.
- Another disadvantage with virtual real estate investing is that it emphasizes short-term thinking. Funding for the long term requires a more extensive picture approach, which may be hard to achieve when you deal with multiple investors at once.

You must understand the risks associated with virtual real estate investing before you dive in. So you can make an informed decision before you begin your journey into this exciting new model of funding.

## The future of virtual real estate investing.

With the rapid development and advancement of technology, virtual real estate investing has quickly become a reality. As it grows, more and more investors can get involved with online real estate investing activities.

As the number of people who choose to invest in this way grows more prominent, it will become easier for others to join in, which means there are plenty of opportunities to profit through investing in virtual real estate.

Virtual investors can now enjoy greater profits and higher returns by investing in countries like the United Kingdom, Canada, etc. You will not be infected by any risks or bad decision-making when investing in virtual real estate, thanks to the technology behind it.

# Chapter 7 How to create, Purchase and sell NFTs

NFTs are an emerging class of assets that can be programmed to have unique properties. They are a blockchain development similar to the NFTs created on the Ethereum Blockchain.

NFTs are digital asset or online currency that the Ethereum project has been developing. NFTs are non-fungible, meaning that they cannot be broken down into smaller parts and cannot be used interchangeably with other assets. Typically, assets such as stocks or bonds can get broken down into smaller pieces and used interchangeably among other assets. NFTs, on the other hand, can never be broken down and can never be interchanged, making them more like a piece of artwork than an investment.

## Development of NFTs

NFTs started being designed in earnest in the latter half of 2017 as the Ethereum Network developed its smart contract and development tools. Ethereum had a tremendous spike in popularity during this time due to the development of both future ERC-721 tokens and an ERC-20 token standard. It became clear that a hybrid solution could be built on this new platform.

In January 2019, CryptoKitties announced that they were partnering with London-based platform RareBits and San Francisco-based game developer Axiom Zen to support the sale and purchase of some of their non-fungible tokens on their platform using fiat currencies.

How to use NFTs

How people will use NFTs in the future is still very uncertain, but there are already some easy ways to use these tokens today that everyone can use regardless of their technical knowledge. Today's cryptocurrencies will likely evolve into their currency, but right now, they are still primarily used as currencies and methods of exchange.

- Purchasing non-fungible tokens from a developer — If you want to use NFTs and don't have the technical knowledge to create your own, you can purchase them from the developers or the exchanges where they are listed. This means that you will have to buy cryptocurrencies first and then exchange them for NFTs through an exchange. This is usually done through a smart contract instead of an automatic process because if anything goes wrong with your transaction, you will need to contact someone from the platform before it can be resolved.

Some platforms allow users to buy directly from their sellers and bypass this step entirely. This enables you to get NFTs immediately and start using them, but it can also mean that you will have to wait longer if there is a backlog of transactions.
- Using non-fungible tokens in games — Most developers who create NFTs will have their games up and running. In some cases, this will involve people buying these NFTs through the platform's smart contract. Still, it isn't uncommon for users to directly trade these tokens between one another without needing to interact with the platform at all.

## How to create NFTs

NFTs can be created using the Ethereum ERC-721 standard. To create a CryptoKitties ERC-721 crypto collectible, you would use the ERC-721 standard and generate a smart contract on the Ethereum blockchain. The creator would then populate this contract with various items, such as artwork and information about the item and its initial price. The creator also needs to include rules and restrictions around how the item can be used.
To create your non-fungible token, you have to have some design and development time available. Creating an NFT is a reasonably involved process with many steps, and each of these steps could benefit from expert help. You'll need to understand how to write smart contracts, make web applications and databases, and do some scripting and programming.
- The first step in creating any NFT is designing the look and feel of your asset, and this requires a strong background in graphic design, although some use cases for NFTs do not require this.
- The second step is to create a smart contract that will hold your specific NFTs. This involves creating valid code that the Ethereum blockchain can read. You can use many difs to store your token type, and some of these contracts have been written specifically for developers who want to learn about and create their own NFTs. The CoinFund has completed two smart contracts: one that is different from an ERC-721 token itself and offers users an easy way to observe whether or not a user has tokens they want but does not require them to generate a new ERC-721 token.
- Once you've decided what type of token you want to create, you will then have to choose how to set up the parameters for that specific NFT, meaning any restrictions on what can be done with your tokens. The creator of the NFT may limit the number or type of transactions that can be performed with this NFT or may even wholly reject transactions from specific addresses or wallets. One needs to decide whether your token will exist in a limited pool, for example with CryptoKitties, where each cat created can only live once and does not provide them with any information about those tokens.

After you've decided on restrictions, it's time to begin populating your smart contract with information, such as what type of artwork and information to use. Your token may also be able to determine its price, although this property is usually reserved for ERC-20 tickets that you can buy and sell in a marketplace.

- The final step before you launch your NFT will be securing it. One of the most significant shortcomings in the CryptoKitties project is that it can be pretty challenging to transmit the ownership of an NFT from one user to another. The creators of CryptoKitties have created a system where you can transfer ownership of your tokens on the Ethereum network but cannot move your tickets to another user. This isn't a massive issue for NFTs that don't require extensive usage, but it can be a problem for collectibles or other types of non-fungible tokens where ownership is essential.

## How to purchase NFTs

There are many different ways to purchase non-fungible tokens, and these methods will vary from game to game (or even from NFT to NFT within the same game). An NF, T can often only be purchased for a specific price in a particular number or through the exchange of other cryptocurrencies. This can be as straightforward as buying tokens directly on a platform or as elaborate as using an open market exchange where anyone can participate.

- Buying directly — Many applications allow users to buy and sell their NFTs directly with the platform itself without having to use another venue or even another cryptocurrency. These transactions can happen by sending a certain amount of tokens to the forum in exchange for the NFT, and the Ethereum network will then handle everything else.

- Buying with a different cryptocurrency — If you have a cryptocurrency that isn't native to the platform, you will have to convert it before using it to purchase an NFT. This means going through an exchange where all of your transactions are handled.

Many users who want to buy non-fungible tokens are more interested in selling their NFTs in the future. Since many non-fungible items cost thousands or even millions of dollars and are unlikely to be used like everyday commodities, most non-fungible tokens that have been created so far are costly thanks to their limited supply, but once people start to use them in games, some people may decide they have outgrown the utility of these tokens and would sell them. This can be a risky proposition because there are no guarantees that the owner will receive a fair price for their NFT.

- Listing on an exchange — In most cases, if you want to sell your NFTs higher in price than you originally purchased them for, then you will need to list them on an exchange where other users can buy from you. This means that you will have to be prepared to wait for an increase in the exchange's price based on demand since no one else will be selling your NFTs and giving you a price.

- Buying from an auction — In rare cases where a single NFT has been created, and there is a large amount of it, users might want to buy the entire supply for their specific token before anyone else. This can take the form of buying NFTs directly from the creator at their price or from those willing to sell at the market rate. This is an easy way to get your hands on NFTs, but it also means that you will have to pay for the entire supply and not just for a portion of it.

## How to sell NFTs

How you sell your non-fungible tokens will depend on how you originally purchased them. You may be able to sell them directly to the platform, or you may need to list them on an exchange, but regardless, you're going to need a bit of information regarding the NFT.

- The first thing that you will need to do is figure out how much your token is worth to determine if it's a good idea to sell or not. Because the price of your token hasn't increased considerably over time, it ca is

the difficult component of selling tokens. Then it might be hard for you to make a profit by selling now (although this can be mitigated by paying lower transaction fees).

- If you are selling directly from the platform, one of the easiest things to do is list it in the buy/sell section of the marketplace under the "non-fungible tokens" category. You can let anyone who wants to buy your token conduct the transaction by sending funds directly to your address and then merging it into the smart contract itself. This gives you a higher chance of receiving more money per token, but you may need to wait for a buyer before conducting your transaction.

If you want to sell non-fungible tokens purchased through another cryptocurrency exchange instead, they will need an extra step before listing them. This involves sending the tickets from your address to the platform to ensure that the platform's smart contract accepts. Some sites will also let you store your non-fungible tokens at a specified location, while others will demand you to send them there.

After the NFTs have been deposited into your account, you can make changes to them (such as setting the price or canceling transactions) and then list them on the exchange to sell them. Ensuring that your NFTs are adequately documented is essential for conducting an essential double-check, and it would be best to double-check what you are selling before listing it.

If you are selling your NFTs on an exchange, you should make sure that the listing is approved first. It will increase your chances of getting a fair
price for your tokens, but you still risk being defrauded or having your transactions rejected.

# Chapter 8 Best New Project and Games in The Metaverse

- SAND

- SAND Project is a game set in a world of floating islands where players can gather resources, build and destroy, explore and discover—using blockchain technology as a backbone to create an entirely new gaming experience. The SAND team is building a platform on which creators from all over the world can collaborate and create new games in a blockchain environment.

- SAND is a decentralized, peer-to-peer economy that allows for the protection of virtual ownership, with the possibility of trading and transacting in the real world. SAND is a digital gaming economy where players can earn, acquire, use and sell in-game resources using Masternodes (controller nodes) based on ERC20 tokens.

- An independent team of game developers will develop the SAND platform and blockchain specialists enthusiastic about gaming. This will help them build games that appeal to generations of gamers and those who understand the technology and how it works.

   o Decentraland (MANA)

- Developed by Decentraland, users will create, experience content, and provide content for others through a decentralized platform. Users can buy land in a virtual world and receive MANA tokens for their land ownership. Then they can monetize their land by renting it out to other people. Landowners have complete control over what happens on their property and set custom rules that must be adhered to if players want to interact with the landowner's property.

- Decentraland is an open-source project that is owned by no single entity. It is governed by its owners, the users of the platform. Everything from the token allocation to defining a set of standard protocols that make up the Decentraland platform will be determined by its community.

   o Nakamoto (NAKA)

- Nakamoto is a decentralized virtual bank that allows you to store your cryptocurrencies without worrying about security breaches and theft. Nakamoto will be built with an in-house bank, which will create its currency. The currency created by the bank will be backed by a reserve of Bitcoin, Ethereum, and other coins. The app is decentralized and aims to provide free banking services at zero cost.

- Players will have the ability to use the Nakamoto platform to trade any asset, including real-world assets, without complex processes and barriers. The Nakamoto team had very early discussions about its platform for trading cryptocurrencies for their fiat currency. This was an essential factor that foreshadowed Nakaomo's future with blockchain technology.

- Metahero (HERO)
- The Metaverse Foundation is a non-profit organization building a blockchain ecosystem using virtual reality technology. It allows people globally to create new virtual worlds with their friends and get paid in cryptocurrency for their virtual and real-life assets. A decentralized marketplace will allow the purchase of virtual assets, but not virtual currency.
- Metahero is an end-to-end decentralized platform that aims to enable individuals, companies, communities, and institutions to create new Virtual Reality worlds with their friends and receive a share of the revenue earned. The Metaverse Foundation is a non-profit organization that includes both a Foundation and an Assembly, responsible for managing the platform's different aspects, including player equity and coin allocation in The Metaverse.
  - o Star Atlas (ATLAS)
- The Team behind Star Atlas is several Slovakian developers who have been developing V.R. games for almost ten years with their studio AtmosGames. AtmosGames was founded in 2014 and has been developing V.R. games since then. Their experiences with V.R. games helped them realize their dream of creating a blockchain-based game.
- At the beginning of 2018, they started the development process of Atlas and created the ATLAS token to be used within Atlas. The team is building a platform that allows users to make and sell virtual spaces for other players to visit a Virtual Reality world to get paid for their content. They aim to provide fair revenue sharing between all creators and users of virtual content and let users take control over their virtual land holdings and movements in any way they see fit.
- Most recently, their team has been collaborating with Chinese partners on the concept of a blockchain integrated game called Dragon Nest (D.N.), released in late 2018. The ATLAS cryptocurrency is the currency used in the game and inside Atlas. The game will allow players to explore and customize virtual spaces while receiving revenue for their creations and activities inside them.
  - o Bloktopia (BLOK)
- Bloktopia is a V.R. game where players can buy, sell, and build lands. The team of six developers is located in Thailand and has been working on Bloktopia for about two years. They try to keep the original concept of Minecraft and develop it into a new reality.

- When players arrive on a new map, their job is to explore it and build any virtual structure they want. Players can fly or walk around the map and go wherever they like. They don't have to worry about encountering dangerous wildlife or other things that might not be safe due to the absence of threat in this virtual world. Creativity and freedom of movement are fundamental concepts in Bloktopia.

- Users will be able to construct or reconstruct anything on the map using a number of construction techniques. Players can sell the creations they built and make a profit from them. All profits from sales are distributed between all the users who created that specific structure; that way, everybody benefits from it in Bloktopia. This is another example of how players are rewarded for their creativity and ingenuity in this game.

  - BlazeBox (BBO)

- BBO is a brand new platform for selling, buying, and trading virtual items from different games at low prices and without restrictions. Expert gamers have developed the platform with decades of experience in online gaming platforms, including Second Life, World of Warcraft, etc. BBO is the world's first universal cryptocurrency platform for buying, selling, and trading in-game items from different games at low prices and without restrictions.

- BBO aims to allow users to trade their virtual items for cryptocurrency whenever and wherever they want. The platform is designed to be easy and very user-friendly. At the moment, there are over 1 billion gamers worldwide who play video games every day. Gamers are constantly growing as game development costs decrease due to modern technologies.

- The main idea behind BBO is to help gamers monetize their in-game experience. The company will solve the problems associated with gaming markets by eliminating intermediaries and allowing users to trade with each other. BBO plans to create a new system completely free of any third-party involvement, helping large and small sellers gain more profit while offering lower prices for buyers. BBO users will be able to buy and sell virtual items at low prices while they get the chance to earn cryptocurrency by providing their services on the platform.

  - Axie Infinity)

- This token is used on the platform to buy virtual pets, purchase virtual items with virtual currencies (virtual currency), and use the voting system while creating new games, levels, or scenarios.

- The project aims to help kids learn how to spend their time wisely and become more responsible individuals in society by allowing them to collect and train virtual pets of different breeds and species, many of which will be unique in their characteristics.

- Kids will train them, socialize and trade with other players. Updates in the game will also be available for purchasing with AXS. As of early 2018, the project has already been in beta testing and has released several new features. The platform's development is almost complete and will be launched officially in mid-2018.

- The Axie Infinity project was created by a team from Italy who had experience working on similar projects, such as "Bubble Island" for Microsoft Kinect and "Peekaboo" for iPhone.


- Highstreet (HIGH)

- Highstreet is a platform for creating and selling virtual items developed by a team from Switzerland. They made the HIGH token to use on the platform and be used in the game itself. The project was launched in July 2017, and they already have several games ready for release and have released more than 30 items, which can be bought with HIGH tokens.

- The main idea behind the Highstreet project is to help players sell their virtual items and craft new items themselves at low prices while receiving profit from their sales. The platform is designed to help gamers profit from their virtual assets and become more active contributors to society via microtransactions rather than passive consumers of virtual goods.

  o Floki Inu (FLOKI)

- Floki Inu is a platform for selling and trading virtual items developed by Germany. The project launched in October 2017 and has about 15 items for sale. They are NPC pets that can be used in the game itself or on other platforms like Facebook, Twitter, and YouTube.

- The main idea behind the Floki Inu project is to help players monetize their in-game experience while meeting new people and receiving profit from the virtual assets that they sell on the platform.

  o Metahero

- Metahero is the world's first blockchain-based ecosystem for building and trading digital collectibles. They have a working beta stage and have released several games, including "Infinity Blade" and "Legacy of Discord." In January 2018, created an in-game marketplace where users can buy and sell their items. They also have an advanced blockchain-based platform for crafting, trading, storing and displaying digital items with ERC721 tokens.

- The project aims to develop a platform where players can easily buy and sell different types of collectibles. Players will b build unique collections at low prices in a safe environment without any worries about fraud or third-party involvement.

- o   Terra Virtua Kolect (

- This is a tokenized ecosystem of games and experiences available on the blockchain, developed by a team from the U.S. It uses V.R. devices to provide players with an authentic virtual reality experience. It focuses on helping users enjoy their time in V.R. using a built-in token system that allows them to buy the relevant content for their interests directly from developers and content producers without any additional costs.

# Chapter 9 Blockchain

## What is blockchain?

Blockchain is an incorruptible digital ledger that provides transparency about its information, including any recordings of financial transactions. Blockchain technology does not require third-party verification since transactions can be added to the blockchain ledger without taking up the storage area on the device making the transaction, which is why blockchain technology doesn't require third-party verification. This has enormous implications for banking and finance because legacy systems like SWIFT don't work with this decentralized model (yet).

Blockchain is the world's most powerful engine for creating value and transforming industries. It can change how businesses operate and interact, taking on various forms across different sectors.

Blockchain was not considered a mainstream technology or even an industry term until recently. That is no longer the case, as many companies are working to integrate this disruptive technology into their business operations without delay.

The potential implications of blockchain are significant enough that it has been deemed one of the top five technologies set to shape our lives in 2018 by Dr. Alex Tapscott, CEO of the Blockchain Research Institute and co-author of Blockchain Revolution. Despite being in its early innings, blockchain has a significant impact on numerous industries, including healthcare, supply chain management, supply chain finance, insurance, and trading finance. This is simple - there are many use cases for blockchain technology.

Blockchain has enormous potential to disrupt financial services and beyond. It can change how we think about identity, digital rights ownership, and payments of all kinds. It can create greater trust and transparency between businesses while at the same time reducing costs associated with verifying transactions. Blockchain can also overhaul many areas of the financial industry - from capital markets to trade finance - without requiring extensive changes or restructuring legacy systems.

Blockchain is safe, and whatever is on them that are encrypted. Even the blockchain's administrators will never update, amend, or erase information kept on the blockchain. This property makes blockchains much more secure than central databases, where systems are vulnerable to hackers who alter or destroy sensitive information. Because of this, blockchain can displace legacy systems and reduce costs associated with the transfer of data - for example, the cost associated with transferring money in and out of banks.

# History of Blockchain

Blockchain was first conceived in 2008 by a person (or persons) known only as Satoshi Nakamoto. Nakamoto founded the bitcoin network, responsible for creating and maintaining blockchain technology and distributing bitcoin. Satoshi's name was never linked to bitcoin, and the identity of this person or group remains unknown.
The first real-world transaction on a blockchain took place in January 2009 when the world's first cryptocurrency – Bitcoin –was sent from one computer to another over the internet. The sender didn't need to provide any personal information because no identification procedures existed yet for making such transactions. In 2016, Alastair Constance wrote in Fortune Magazine that "Bitcoin is haunting Wall Street.
Currently, there are more than 100,000 blockchain developers in the world. These are people responsible for creating organizations and companies that utilize blockchain in their day-to-day operations.

# How does Blockchain Work?

In general, transactions on the blockchain are public, traceable, and unchangeable. This means they can be verified easily by anyone, allowing anyone to create a secure audit trail of transactions in a specific asset or currency using the blockchain. However, there is not enough information to link identities with individual transactions on the network conclusively. Since there aren't any central authorities controlling the blockchain, users control it directly. For this reason, users can confirm that their transactions are valid and are not being tampered with by another user. A record made on the blockchain and signed off by a user cannot be altered without altering all subsequent blocks.

# Uses of Blockchain;

Blockchain's ledger technology can manage numerous functions of the financial industry. In the case of the banking industry, it can replace the need for a centralized database that would be easier to manipulate. Also,
since a central database contains all credit card and personal information at once, someone who hacks that database could potentially steal money or credit card information. Since no central authority verifies transactions in blockchain networks, hackers cannot pass identity data or perform fraudulent transactions.
Blockchain has many uses beyond financial transactions – such as tracking elections, creating digital records, validating copyright and proof of authorship, and reducing fraud in real estate markets.

Distributed Ledger Technology and the blockchain

It is a ledger that records cryptocurrency transactions. It is powered by participants who log in to the Blockchain network and record transactions. This recording method adds a system of trust to the relationship between multiple users, removing the need for intermediaries in many cases. The cryptographic nature of the blockchain allows for anonymous ownership, meaning that anyone can record themselves as the owner of any particular block of data to be trusted or proven authentic. This data can then be shared or transmitted with others on the network beyond its origins.

It is useful where you cannot trust your partner. For example, a business or an investor can use blockchain to gain products, services, or finannot registered on the trade register (or other databases). This can be useful for businesses that need to get unregistered goods for resale or for companies that directly offer unregulated ducts to the public. Blockchain-derived cryptocurrency is also helpful when a central authority cannot be trusted.

## Types of blockchains

There are many different kinds of blockchains: public (peers who can read and write to it), private (only administrators or owners), permissioned (made to work in concert with other similar databases), hybrid (a combination of each).

1. Public - anyone can read and write to it.

Public blockchains are ideal when you want everyone to participate in the resource or activity you are sharing. For example, if you want everyone to see documents or payments, a public blockchain is likely the best choice. A private blockchain is the most secure option to control it. On a public blockchain like Bitcoin, individual users have no privacy features.

1. Private - administrators can control who has access, how much, and for how long

Private blockchains are ideal when you restrict the number of participants in a network. It is helpful for organizations or groups with limited members and needs to control their access, and this can be achieved by using an identity system like uPort. These blockchains are also called consortium or federated because they're usually created by for-profit companies and run internally.

1. Permissioned - members need to agree on the rules and work together.

Permissioned blockchains are ideal when you want members to control data access. They are often used in companies and organizations with
strict regulations or corporate governance requirements. This is typically achieved by bringing together member institutions that desire to share information but want to maintain some measure of control over how that information is shared. For example, banks may wish their transaction information to be visible only on internal networks.

Hybrid - a combination of each

Hybrid blockchains are not entirely one but have public and private protocol elements. For instance, a blockchain can be created so that transactions are publicly visible in real-time, but the ledger is only shared with select members. Another example would be a private blockchain between a large company and its vendors and suppliers. These blockchains would require approval from one or more administrators and must be ratified by each organization's governing body before any changes are made to the distributed ledger.

However, all blockchains share certain standard features that are the foundation for their disruptive potential across industries: trust, speed, and security.

- Trust

Blockchain technology is a peer-to-peer system that doesn't require intermediaries (e.g., banks or a government) to verify and process transactions. Because of this, it's much faster and can eliminate the risk of human error by making these transactions more secure and less susceptible to fraud and theft.

- Speed

Blockchain offers the ability to transfer value between two parties in near real-time, with the added benefit of increased security because each block is linked in a chronological way that cannot be altered.

- Security

Security is one of blockchain's most important characteristics and arguably the primary reason for its popularity. Each block contains a record of all transactions that have ever occurred in the system, making it nearly impossible to change one piece of information without affecting the entire trade. This makes it virtually impossible to alter records without being caught by others in the system, which eliminates human error and fraud.

## Why should I adopt a blockchain strategy?

Blockchain affects the way we do business in just about every industry, and Companies need to start thinking about how they can incorporate this emerging technology into their plans. Here are just a few reasons why:

- Reduced costs

Blockchain transactions are faster, cheaper, and more secure than those of legacy systems to which we've become accustomed. This means businesses can make more money without losing out on valuable savings.

- Increased transparency

A blockchain keeps track of every transaction in the system, making it easier to maintain transparency and accountability. In this way, businesses can make better decisions about products and services based on their customers' needs rather than simply relying on their internal data.

- Increased security

Blockchain transactions are more secure than those made using legacy systems because they are not subject to human error. For example, using a blockchain system can help reduce the risk of identity theft because each transaction is recorded directly in a distributed ledger, which cannot be altered without altering all other blocks on the chain.

- Smart contracts

This legally binding contract often between two parties allows them to transfer money and make other promises that would be difficult or impossible to fulfill with standard contracts. Smart contracts allow for automatic payments when certain conditions are met by two parties and eliminate the need for third-party verification.

Transaction types

Blockchain can be used to transfer any information or value between two parties, be it digital currencies like Bitcoin or cryptocurrencies. Blockchain has been used as an underlying technology (e.g., Ethereum) to facilitate cryptocurrency transactions without requiring users to interact with a third-party service provider (such as a bank).

## What's Next for Blockchain?

The future of blockchain is inspiring, and we can see the possibilities growing all the time. There are many questions about blockchain technology, and it isn't easy to know where to begin.

# Chapter 10 Metaverse and Cryptocurrency;

Metaverse is a platform to explore various aspects of virtual reality. It also facilitates digital transactions for digital assets and creates its currency, ETP.

Since its debut in February, the ETP price has grown by approximately 300%. But it wasn't until September that it began to experience the rate of growth many cryptocurrencies have seen. This was thanks to BTCC announcing that it would start allowing trading in ETP on September 20. Later that month, Metaverse announced a significant upgrade to its blockchain platform, and the main net went live on September 29.

Cryptocurrency makes use of cryptography to safeguard financial transactions and the creation of new units. It is a decentralized currency hence it does not belong to any particular country or government. While developers are often associated with cryptocurrency, it is essential to remember several other roles involved in the ecosystem. These jobs include miners, traders, exchanges, wallets, and merchants.

Regardless of the various roles involved in cryptocurrency, developers are typically responsible for creating wallets so that users can store their coins. They also develop platforms to facilitate trading between currencies and assets. Companies that are making their tokens are also in need of developers. These tokens can be used to pay for services on a new platform or traded and held as an investment. The company issues the permit to investors in exchange for money or capital.

A big part of cryptocurrency is the mining process. Mining involves proof of work when computers solve complex math problems to help
secure the network by approving transactions. The computer that solves these problems first receives a reward for its efforts, often more coins for its owner. The proof of work process has become incredibly difficult due to the number of miners trying to crack it every day.

The recent drop in mining difficulty has led to one mining pool of 51 percent majority, essentially solving all the problems. This has allowed them to control the creation of new bitcoin, which is currently at a record high value of $11,300 per coin. With this control, They can move money away from traditional markets and into bitcoin.

Cryptocurrency came pretty early, but the digital currency era is not even close to over. Blockchain has been used for other purposes, but it was always about borderless currency and payments. Metaverse is trying to change that and make valuable blockchain for non-currency-based digital assets.

One of the issues for digital currencies is that there is a lot of inefficient record keeping. Digital currency owners have to keep track of everything because it can be used everywhere, from online to in-person. The issue could be solved with blockchain technology, but as Metaverse pointed out, it's not that easy when looking at other business models.

The big problem with digital currency is that there are no actual use cases yet (after all, they are still very early). Blockchain technology has a great potential aside from just currency.

Metaverse uses a proof of work mechanism but doesn't mine or generate new tokens. The currently available supply of ETP is 100 million, out of

which roughly 75 million ETP are already in circulation. The free market determines the value of ETP, and currently, the value of 1 ETP stands at USD 1,88.

Metaverse and Cryptocurrency work together to provide easy access to people, and they are both parts of the blockchain, and this is just the beginning of it. Metaverse and Cryptocurrency are terms used in a definite sense, so it is essential to know the exact meaning of both words.

For better understanding, let's take an example:

If a person buys stock from someone who does not have any paper to prove that he owns these stocks, this transaction cannot be considered legal. To make it legal, a third party can take an appointment from both the parties that these stocks will be stored in his safe custody to be used as proof at any time later if need be. This third party is called Custodian.

Metaverse was built on top of Ethereum's blockchain, and its token ETP was launched in 2016. The blockchain platform enables users to store their identity data and see it used by different websites throughout the internet. Users can create decentralized applications (DApps) within Metaverse and for cryptocurrencies. An ETP is a token that is used to raise funds for projects, as well as to buy virtual assets from other users on The Metaverse platform. The Cryptocurrency Metaverse(ETP)" has its blockchain, which works with Ethereum's smart contract. As a result of this, the co-founders of Metaverse see an excellent future for this currency. The value of ETP fluctuates according to market conditions in both markets.


Cryptocurrencies could be implemented into various sectors such as the financial market, telecommunications, security, and the Internet of Things (IoT). Blockchain technology could be applied in supply chain management, for example, to track goods and materials. This would result in reduced time for production lines as well as enabling low-cost global transactions."

There is a massive potential for cryptocurrency to become mainstream and even replace traditional currencies as a of legal tender of trade in the future. Similarly, there is also considerable potential for Blockchain technology to revolutionize many areas of different sectors worldwide.

# Features of Metaverse and Cryptocurrency;

- Metaverse is a platform to explore various aspects of virtual reality. It also facilitates digital transactions for digital assets and creates its currency, ETP.

- The value of ETP fluctuates according to market conditions in both markets.

- The co-founders of Metaverse see an excellent future for this currency.

- Reliable and robust Blockchain

- Digital assets storage on Blockchain

Metaverse and Cryptocurrency relate in that they are both blockchain-based projects. Metaverse has created its cryptocurrency, ETP, the native currency on The Metaverse blockchain. This unique combination of a
decentralized exchange and a stable coin could be needed to create a new future for this industry.

The team at Metaverse has managed to identify and solve many of the problems present in other digital currencies and blockchain platforms.

The Metaverse project has been developing for over four years. The platform is fully loaded with various features such as: "wallet, explorer, Renko charts, blockchain explorer, and voting. It also boasts an extensive set of APIs to allow developers to create new blockchain-based applications." The development team has created a platform that allows them to interact with the Ethereum Virtual Machine (EVM), which will enable developers to interact with smart contracts. This means that any new Metaverse blockchain-based applications will have access to the benefits that Ethereum has created over the last few years.

# How Metaverse and cryptocurrency differ.

- Metaverse is a digital asset application platform based on blockchain technology. Cryptocurrency is a digital currency system based on cryptographic technologies for trading and payment.

- Based on the blockchain consensus mechanism, Metaverse produces Dapp, smart contract, and digital assets circulation system to match the demand for various applications of Blockchain; cryptocurrency aims to become an alternative payment method to replace traditional paper money.

- Metaverse provides an open-source, public Blockchain protocol and digital asset management tool to create an ecosystem of value exchange. Cryptocurrency emphasizes privacy protection and aims to be used as a means of settlement.

The future of Metaverse and Cryptocurrency

Network capacity: data storage, transaction speed, and computational efficiency. These are key factors that determine the value of cryptocurrency. Blockchain is an efficient way of storing data thanks to the blockchain architecture, which securely holds large amounts of data models. As other technological innovations such as 3D3D printing and artificial intelligence have been developed in recent years, blockchain has become more efficient due to its decentralized nature. This enables faster transactions with less energy consumption and a lower cost than traditional payment systems. The power-saving capabilities of the Blockchain have resulted from the fact that it minimizes the need for intermediaries in various parts of our daily lives, such as banking and payments. Metaverse blockchain has 1000 transactions per second (TPS) transaction processing capability, which is higher than Bitcoin, which can handle 7 TPS. Metaverse currently does not have the technical capabilities to support large-scale commercial applications, but the team has plans shortly. They aim to increase transaction speeds and processing times to enable them to support mainstream applications."

The transaction time for Bitcoin is about 10 minutes, and for Ethereum, it's about 20 seconds. Blockchain technology has a few people who own most of the tokens, while other Cryptocurrencithe es controls a single entity.

Previously, cryptocurrencies have been in the spotlight for their rapid increase in value. As a result of this, there has been a massive increase in interest for them across the globe. This has resulted in many companies starting to trade in this currency. Its success has resulted from some countries adopting them as a legaltenders, such as Japan which accepts Bitcoin payments. We shall see metaverse and cryptocurrency expand and gain popularity worldwide in the following years.

# Chapter 11 The Altcoin

## What is the Altcoin?

(Alternative coins)

The altcoin is a name for all cryptocurrencies other than Bitcoin.

Altcoins work like Bitcoin: transactions are made and stored in a public ledger (a blockchain), and the power to create new coins is distributed proportionately. The critical difference between an Altcoin and Bitcoin is that Altcoins may offer different features or improvements over Bitcoins- such as anonymity or faster transaction times.

Excluding the first few Altcoins created as novelty items, many were released as what can be best described as a political protest against centralization, such as those resulting from single administrators or developers controlling software updates that dictate network protocol rules, which become unchangeable after being accepted by a majority of nodes on the network.

Bitcoin has one problem: it doesn't have any actual use. It used to be a currency, but there's no reason for anyone to use it because it's useless except to buy drugs from the Silk Road. So what we need is an alternative currency.

I can only assume that the Community doesn't want Altcoins because they're not using them. That's fine; altcoins aren't helpful either, so there is no danger there.

But why would use for them be so limited?

There is no reason to use Bitcoin. Yes, I know it's the most popular and well-known altcoin, but it's unnecessary. If you can't use it, no one will force you to. So instead of an alternative currency, we'll call this the Political Coin.

What if we make a coin that is not just another currency but a revolutionary new way of thinking about money? A coin that rejects fiat money and our flawed notion of what money is altogether.

The Altcoin has no chains. If you have Altcoins, you do not need to use Bitcoin because it is simply a tool for exchanging one Altcoin for another. You can hold them or trade them. The Altcoin does not require you to trust anyone to render the system stable or secure. By handing over that authority and printing the financial corporations and governments, who are ultimately interested in keeping you silent, you don't have to give up your independence or power as an individual participant in the system.

# History of Altcoin.

The development of Altcoins has followed a timeline similar to the Bitcoin timeline. However, since there have been more Altcoins than Bitcoins, this timeline focuses slightly differently.

Altcoins began as white papers with ideas that had not yet been implemented in code, hence the term "concepts." There was no code at the time, and it wouldn't be until many months later, when developers began working on this algorithm, all of these concepts would lead to

actual functional coins. As the community grew and people came up with new ideas, the Altcoin mailing list was born.

In July of 2012, this mailing list was created to unite people from different Altcoins to share knowledge and innovation. The index remains active today, and many coins have up to a hundred people on the mailing list helping to develop them. This gave rise to new coins like Litecoin, Namecoin, and SolidCoin. Eventually, new coins would carry more advanced technical improvements over older ones, and the developer communities would split away to found their Altcoin. This became known as "forking" in the Altcoin community, where an existing project spawns a new one.

High-profile developers precisely did some of these forks because they thought the older coin was falling into disrepair. For example, Litecoin was forked from Bitcoin for this reason, and many see it as an improvement over its progenitor because Bitcoin's dif retargeting period is too long. Although the various threads for these Altcoins are active, some have never really gained traction with developers or users, even though they provided new applications built on the core concepts of cryptocurrency like Ripple or Freicoin.

# Types of Altcoins.

1. One-Click Altcoin
 Like Bitcoin, this coin has an open-source algorithm and does not require any special knowledge or effort to work with. The main difference is that for an Altcoin to be considered "one-click," you must
have a wallet set up with a client that works with the currency.

2. Capped Coin
An alternate form of Altcoin where a maximum of 1,000 coins are allowed per wallet at the time of creation or last transaction. In mint coin, this value was set at 20,000 coins during its inception but has since been changed to 0 coins, so all new wallets have their unique number to prevent mining on multiple nodes.

3. Indie Coin

This one-click Altcoin is unique because it has no premise or IPO. Both are typically used in alternative currencies to generate demand before the developer issues the coin. Indie Coins usually have a funding goal with a predetermined cap that must be reached to create the cash. This way, developers have an idea of how many coins they need and can work towards that goal without dealing with too many untested ideas.

4. Mint Coin

An alternative form of Altcoin was newly created wallets starting "minted" with a maximum number of coins, called the "minting cap. "

5. Premine Coin

An Altcoin that differs from the Indie Coin in that once a hard-coded number of coins have been created, the developer does not give them to anyone for free. Instead, they are given to people who helped develop it, and everyone else gets nothing.

6. Pump and Dump Coin

This form of Altcoin is for everyone who wants to get rich quickly. It's called the Pump and Dump because it involves buying up the coin with a group of friends and then selling it off to make a quick profit once the price is high enough.

## Applications of the Altcoin

- Altcoins are used to transfer money just like Bitcoin: you can use a small amount from your account to buy something from someone else's account. - You can use Altcoins for speculation, just like Bitcoin: you can buy a mining contract for 1 BTC, then immediately sell the bitcoin at the market rate.

- Altcoins are used to transact data faster, like Bitcoin, and specifically, they allow anyone to transfer information more quickly than Bitcoin offers. For example, imagine a payment system that took ten minutes to send an email; with an Altcoin like Namecoin, you could send that email in less than.

- Some Altcoins offer more anonymity than others, and some have better privacy features than others. The anonymity that Altcoins provide comes at a cost. While Bitcoin has proven to be secure, many Altcoins have not, and some coins charge a transaction fee for each transaction you make, as well as for each block through which your transaction passes data.

- Altcoins are used to create faster products and services that Bitcoin cannot. They are much more flexible and innovative than Bitcoin and more valuable, as they have features like integrated anonymous messaging and distributed storage that Altcoin users can take advantage of.

- Altcoins are used to create new services that Bitcoin cannot: imagine a distributed mortgage service that no longer requires you to trust the person you are doing business with or a decentralized stock market. Or imagine an utterly anonymous currency like Monero or Dash.
- Altcoin is used to create faster products and services that Bitcoin is not capable of: imagine decentralized email servers or instant messaging services on top of IPFS, an alternative to HTTP.

# The Future of Altcoin

The future of Altcoins looks bright because many people share the same sentiment on how we perceive currency and trade in our daily lives. The focus on community and decentralization makes Altcoins the perfect choice for future development. As the demand for currency and business grows, Altcoin can grow with it.

If we can show that our economy cannot be controlled, we would expand privacy and freedom into every aspect of our lives. Imagine a nation where everyone had a voice and not just the wealthy elite; imagine
a world where people could choose how they spend their time and with whom they spend it. The decisions made in today's economy will determine what happens tomorrow and if you believe that your future should be in your own hands. Join us on the Altcoin journey.

This has created an economy where thousands of people actively trade coins every day; most people don't even see it as an investment, and Altcoins have become a reality. This also means that there is a genuine chance that a new coin could replace Bitcoin or Ethereum, depending on how well it gets implemented and how secure it becomes. Altcoin's future depends on what users are willing to put into them; if you feel like your coin has a lot, you should support it by holding it and using it with other people. If your cash offers unique features, then keep them because you might be helping other people think outside the box as well.

Many in the cryptocurrency community saw the Altcoin massive bust cycle as ahu,e failure, especially those affected most. However, there are many reasons to have faith in the future of Altcoin; cryptocurrency is an innovative market, and if Altcoin is ever to beat out Bitcoin or Ethereum, then it will be because of these innovative features. We learn from the previous busts that coins with real value survive and are only strengthened by a crash like this. Fortunately for supporters of Altcoin developers are not giving up just yet. We should expect innovations and exciting changes to Altcoins in years to come.

# Altcoin Threats.

Altcoins are threatened similarly to Bitcoin; developers create them, and they often die away after they are created. However, Altcoin holders have adapted over time by producing more features to their coins and making them more practical to trade with. It poses a threat to the currency economy because it can be a cheap alternative to Bitcoin, and people have demonstrated that they prefer it over Bitcoin.

Recently there has been a rise in Altcoin; new Altcoins are being created every day, some of which are incredibly interesting. The main threat to Altcoins is their users; people can copy the Bitcoin code and place it in their Altcoin, then they will have an identical product. Even if they do not use all of the features, they may still attract new users who want a product like Bitcoin. The Future of Altcoin

# Chapter 12 How to Invest in Bitcoin and Altcoin

Just like any other investment, trading Altcoin and Bitcoin involves risks. It is possible that Bitcoin will become too expensive to buy or one day be worth very little in the future. If you're serious about investing in these autonomous digital currencies, you will need to research which cryptocurrencies are good choices and why they should be invested into. This can be accomplished by reading up on cryptocurrency blogs and forums for expert opinions concerning which coins are in demand at this moment in time.

## How to Buy Altcoins:

1. Determine the percentage of your crypto portfolio dedicated to altcoin- 25% is generally considered an excellent percentage to allocate to altcoins as you want to afford the swings in the market when it comes to altcoins.
2. Identify which coins are most promising and invest accordingly-
The ones that looked like they would be the next big thing, or those getting good numbers of investors into the cryptocurrency community are usually worth looking into first. Some of these currencies, especially Ethereum and Litecoin, have increased massively in value over the last year. If you have a lot of money in your cryptocurrency wallet, you can always spend all of it on one coin and wait for it to increase significantly over time (with support).
3. Only invest in altcoins that you believe will bring a long-term profit if they increase value. You can make a nice profit from any cryptocurrency predicted to do well in the future, but you need to have patience.
4. Do Your research and don't over-invest. It is not the goal of the altcoin market to make you a millionaire. It is simply a quick and easy way to move your money into a new form of currency (cryptocurrency). Something must be in it for you to keep clinging on.. This means that you need to research each altcoin before investing in them. In most cases, your research will lead you back to the same few coins predicted by many individuals like Coinmarket cap and Coinigy.
5. Do not invest over invest
Many people make this mistake when investing in altcoins. Many people spend all of their savings on one coin only to see it drop in value by 50% within a few weeks. Being keen on the value of your holdings so you could stay well away from danger zones where a sudden drop in weight could significantly affect your portfolio.
6. Do not invest in an altcoin that a hacked platform has -

What does this mean? If a coin has been created and gained popularity on a platform like Bitcointalk Organisation which has now become riddled with hackers or phishers, you mustn't use it as your primary source of research.

7. Start small and make your way up-

You should never invest all of your hard-earned money into one cryptocurrency. Try and start small with a few altcoins that you believe

will increase in value, to begin with. This is a good way for you to get your feet wet in the world of cryptocurrency, but at the same time, it will have a limited effect on your bank account. For your investment to appreciate over time, you will need to ensure that you put enough money into each coin to make it worthwhile.

## How to buy Bitcoins

1. Use sites like Coinbase to buy bitcoins; you do not have to buy a whole Bitcoin and start small with USD 10.

2. If you want to go the more traditional route, then you can research online what your local coin club has to offer, or even consider a visit to a local coin dealer's office where staff can help you with the process of purchasing your Bitcoins in person. Many new people to cryptocurrencies find this a more secure way of buying the currency.

3. You can also use sites like shapeshift to buy altcoins through bitcoin-

Although the process is not quite the same, it works similarly. This type of site lets you exchange cryptocurrency in your portfolio for a different digital currency that you prefer, but with one difference. It does not require you to hold on to any funds for an arbitrary amount of time before you can use them as you want. The exchange process is instant, and if there is anything that you do not like about the current trading conditions, you have to wait for a few minutes before they change again.

4. Do not keep all of your funds in one place-

Some people like to store their bitcoins on their computers or perhaps on USB sticks. This is a good way to keep an eye on things, it is also

hazardous if your laptop is lost or stolen. To save your funds you can do is spread out the funds over several wallets on the internet and then give them access to as many addresses as possible. It is also a good idea for you to back up your data frequently and even consider putting passwords on the wallets in online locations so that no one else can access them unless they know the password.

5. Be sure to use a wallet that a reputable company has created.

Many fake wallets claim to be legitimate on the internet but are nothing more than scams designed to steal your funds. To determine if your wallet is legit is to download its official mobile app so that you will always have access and can keep an eye on your investments at any one time. Someone else cannot manage your fund in paper wallet since only give access to those who have special access and know the password.

6. Do not keep coins in exchanges for longer than you need to-
Exchanges like Bittrex and Poloniex are popular amongst people new to crypto, but they can be riskier than they appear. many people have been victims to hacking at these exchanges, and once your account contained inside them has been hacked, then you should be prepared for it to disappear forever. Whatever happens, do not deposit more cash into an exchange account once it has been hacked; you will simply be making more money for the hacker. If anything does happen, inform the authorities as soon as possible to begin a legal investigation into the case.

7. Do not keep your coins in a wallet that has been lost or destroyed-
If you are thinking about buying large amounts of cryptocurrency, it is
good to have a backup of your wallet. Some people who have lost their wallets have been forced to transfer all their money to another exchange because they could no longer access their original account. You must maintain an online version of your bitcoin wallet - if someone happens to steal it, then they would not have access to the bitcoin that is stored inside the online version.

8. Do not keep your coins on a computer that is infected with essential
You must ensure that your computer is clean and virus accessible before making any transfers. The moment you install any software on a computer that can contain viruses, it becomes infected with them, and then they can be used to steal Bitcoins from your wallet. It is also a good idea for you to ensure that you are using an antivirus so that any threats have been dealt with before they have time to do damage.

9. Do not send coins somewhere where the person collecting them does not live-
The moment that someone else receives your bitcoins and gives themselves access to use them is when things can go downhill fast for you.

## Risks of investing in Bitcoins and Altcoins

- The risk of being hacked
Since there is a lot of money in cryptocurrency now, hackers are always looking for new ways to intrude into secure systems and steal your investment. While certain websites have been known to be fully closed
as it relates to hacking. The best way to protect yourself from this type of threat is to use storage devices containing bitcoins and not keep them online. You can also ask other people invested in cryptocurrency to confirm if a website is legitimate before using it.

- Being the victim of a phishing attack-

This type of threat can affect you if you are new to crypto. People will often send emails to investors or companies claiming to be official representatives of various exchanges, which ask them for information or, in some cases, ask them for money. You should never disclose any personal data like your long number, email address, or even your credentials linked to an exchange - this can all be used by hackers to steal everything you have.

- The devaluation of the currency-

The most crucial fact about cryptocurrencies is that they face extreme volatility daily. This means that you can wake up one day and find that the value of your investment has dropped by 10% just because of market fluctuations. If you are investing in cryptocurrency purely to make extra money, this can be frustrating and cause you to lose out on the money you are trying to earn. While it is true that the value of bitcoin has reached record levels in 2018, doesn't guarantee its stability for long.

- The risk of very high fees-

Bitcoin transactions involve a very high fee because special services have to be employed so that bitcoin miners can have an incentive for their work. In some cases, you may have to pay a high fee just so that you can

transfer money to another wallet or exchange. There is no way for you to avoid these fees - the only thing you can do is research into any funds you need to invest and make sure that the page is not full of hidden charges that will eat up your profits.

- The risk of not knowing anything-

If you're new to cryptocurrencies, you might discover that the information you have access to is either incomplete or, in some circumstances, deliberately incorrect. This means that it may be difficult for you to gain any real insight into how it works, and then when investment opportunities pop up such as ICOs - you may struggle to know which one is worth investing in. If there are no reliable sources of information available to you, it could be easy for another person to try and take advantage of your lack of knowledge.

# Chapter 13 Business opportunities in Metaverse

Depending on your creativity, you can make a fortune from your knowledge of cryptocurrencies and the crypto world.

The opportunities to explore the new technology and introduce its integration into the daily lives of people are endless.

On the one hand, there are plenty of areas that are still unexplored and can quickly become the focal points of further development:

There is a constant need for new ideas, approaches, and solutions that could help resolve. Metaverse offers a wide range of opportunities in the modern-day world. It explores the new technologies and the challenges as some of these tools can be used for conflict.

Metaverse will take part in the revolution of blockchain technology as demonstrated through The Metaverse's strong ICO performance.

Depending on your creativity, you can make a fortune from your knowledge of cryptocurrencies and the crypto world.

The opportunities to explore the new technology and introduce its integration into the daily lives of people are endless.

On the one hand, there are plenty of areas that are still unexplored and can quickly become the focal points of further development:

There is a constant need for new ideas, approaches, and solutions that could help resolve current issues in different industries. Blockchain technology is an excellent solution for traditional finance, trade, politics, art, gaming, and many other spheres.

New tools and services can be created using existing blockchain technologies that support opportunities for vast communities worldwide.

But some issues must be solved such as data protection, copyright, and other important matters. In these areas, we are making preparations to address these issues.

Metaverse is one of the most important projects in blockchain technology which is unique and with a long-lasting future.

Metaverse's advanced technology solutions have been followed by an increasing number of users and investors. With the introduction of a new Bitcoin mining chip, metaverse is rapidly becoming the world's first parallel blockchain software construction platform. In addition to our solid technical value and rapid development, metaverse's plan for far-sighted social design and economic innovation is also under scrutiny.

The blockchain system has entered into the information age, and we are seeing the birth of a new era that transcends communication, storage, and trading.

Some of the opportunities in metaverse are;

Buying transaction fees from metaverse to any other blockchain.

It is done by providing the "bridge" service, which guarantees to pay any transaction fee on another blockchain in metaverse for others while the other blockchain is not live.

Priority blockchain trading

Metaverse recognizes the value of being a "priority blockchain," but metaverse is not just aiming at being ranked number one. We also acknowledge that essential features could not be achieved long-term if only two or three blockchains. Metaverse will cooperate with other blockchains and build a bridge to transfer digital assets among different blockchain networks. They want to carry out an exclusive service for those who want to buy and sell digital assets between other blockchains or serve as a mediator for digital asset transfer. Users can send digital assets to The Metaverse's wallet, and it will initiate a transaction to the destination of their choice promptly.

Digital asset distribution

Speculative demand and market supply, which are decided by investors' willingness to buy tokens, currently drive the price of most blockchain assets. However, these factors alone do not reflect the value of the blockchain resources, especially for metaverse blockchains or other blockchain-based projects. Digital assets such as Bitcoin exist only in a blockchain network, with value reflected in speculative demand and supply factors. The entire coin circulation only reflects 1 million units in circulation, but that does not mean there are 1 million units with intrinsic value.

Digital asset identification certification

Metaverse is not a public institution, and there is neither a central authority nor an intermediary that can verify the authenticity of all digital assets issued by metaverse. Without a standard mechanism to verify such

realism, it will be challenging to determine whether the digital asset in hand has value and is authentic. Metaverse's registered certification mark on the blockchain network. The users can see through Metaverse Explorer (or other similar tools) and search for the certified address of certification body, which can help users distinguish between fake and genuine digital assets by scanning the blockchain itself, which is an easy way to solve this problem.

Digital asset data certification

Data certification is another important yet less developed application within blockchain technology, especially within the context of digital assets. Metaverse will support this by providing a service to certify data on the blockchain network. There are two applications in this area: first, to provide authentication certification of data on the blockchain network and second, to create a reliable data certification application within the blockchain.

The first application will be used to establish a standard mechanism for digital asset classification. It will be used as a verification instrument of digital assets that can help users determine whether the digital asset is genuine or not. Metaverse will provide authorized certification through its certified third party partners.

Metaverse believes that external data certification is an important part of business intelligence in the future, especially in trade and financial solutions, which require accurate and timely information from other trusted sources.

## Market creation

Metaverse provides a platform for the future economy and society construction based on open source to develop an alternative economic and social system. Metaverse does not have any specific goals in mind for its own business. Still, it trusts that the masses can understand and cooperate according to their creativity when creating development opportunities in the future or marketing opportunities in the present.

The Metaverse Foundation encourages different market players (such as financial institutions, technology companies, law-making organizations, and individuals) to develop relevant services. The Foundation will offer its help to develop these services, and hopefully, everyone can cooperate and make a win-win situation together.

## Digital assets management service platform

Many people used to keep their hard cash or gold in their safes or deposit boxes at home, but no one would prefer to keep their digital assets this way. More extensive asset management usually requires a higher security infrastructure, risk control mechanism, professional interpretation, and advanced system maintenance. This is why we will gradually develop and offer an asset management service platform to carefully manage digital assets, taking security as the first priority. We believe that the development of this service will be in the highest demand in such a digital asset ecosystem.


## Blockchain Operating System

As blockchain technology is further developed, its applications will inevitably increase and infill every aspect of our lives. Therefore, there is a considerable rate potential market for the blockchain operating system. People do not only want to apply blockchain technology. They also want to use blockchain technology in ways that make sense. The blockchain operating system will be the core of the Metaverse ecosystem.

Although there are many different types of blockchain projects, each with its own characteristics, they all share a desire to create something new. While blockchains are often used for financial and digital asset transactions, Metaverse hopes to push for greater application of this technology in other areas of our daily lives as well.

There is no doubt that we have gone through an explosive technological and monetary development over the past decade.

## Publicity and promotion platform

The primary purpose of metaverse's publicity and promotion platform is to promote the development of The Metaverse Ecosystem. It will provide a variety of publicity and promotion tools for core companies within the industry, such as metaverse.

It will also offer more tools and resources for users to share content, such as:

## Digital Asset Management Service Platform

The value of the digital assets issued by Metaverse should reflect the value of Metaverse itself and its community.

Therefore, it is essential to identify risks and rewards on a blockchain network based on the economic relationship between users and developers. The Metaverse Foundation believes that breakthrough solutions to address the issue of digital asset management will be discovered in the future.

Metaverse Foundation Operations

The Metaverse Foundation operates based on a nonprofit organization, and it will control the foundation's assets and have a public's fiduciary responsibility. The role of the Metaverse Foundation will be to develop the ecosystem according to its own preset development direction, and seek other potential applications of blockchain technology in various areas of society. The foundation hopes that different forces can cooperate with it to promote the development of digital assets in direct relation to other industries, including finance, law, management, etc., so that all participants can compete within a fair environment.

Blockchain-based AI system (project name: META)

The blockchain-based AI system is a project of Artificial Intelligence-based on blockchain technology. Its purpose is to provide an innovative strategy to realize the connection between human and artificial intelligence using blockchain technology. It's helpful in digital asset management, identity verification, digital copyright certification, and other intelligent applications.

Digital asset exchange platform (project name: VMS)

The Metaverse Foundation is currently working with different partners to develop a digital asset exchange based on The Metaverse blockchain, which is expected to be released in 2018. Now, the development team is focusing on designing the trading interface, which includes both web and mobile versions. The Metaverse Foundation will continue to provide updates to community members throughout the development progress.

Other Blockchain applications for business opportunities.

The development team of Metaverse Foundation will also undertake other blockchain-based solutions that can be developed in parallel to match the needs of different industries and business scenarios.

Metaverse Blockchain Application

Metaverse is a public institution that integrates blockchain technology into cross-border value chains to build an open and shared digital certificate platform that can bring prosperity to people worldwide and extend to new markets and industries.

Metaverse offers a large pool of business opportunities, including but not limited to digital asset trading, blockchain-based digital identity management, and token issuing services. It is still early, but the roadmap is laid out nicely and clear for the community to follow.

The creative entrepreneurs are presented with the opportunity to disrupt the financial markets, define new business models, and create new markets. They can make money by providing their unique value-added service or products to the users within The Metaverse ecosystem

The Metaverse Foundation does not own any equity shares of the organizations it sponsors or funds, and the Metaverse Foundation also holds all digital assets issued by these organizations. The purpose of The Metaverse Foundation is to provide support to its sponsored companies and individuals following their individual needs, whether financial or technical.

Looking at these opportunities, Metaverse Foundation has developed its vision to help build a blockchain open-source ecosystem to revitalize the current system.

current issues in different industries. Blockchain technology is an excellent solution for traditional finance, trade, politics, art, gaming, and many other spheres.

New tools and services can be created using existing blockchain technologies that support opportunities for vast communities worldwide.

# Chapter 14 10 Business Models in Metaverse

The Metaverse world has brought many business opportunities for experienced and novice entrepreneurs. It is not just about coding or creating a game, and it can be used to create anything you want from your imagination. The success of metaverse is dependent on the players. You can earn money from virtual properties or be imaginative in creating new content or games. You can still generate revenue from it as long as you have a good concept and the willingness to work.

Metaverse came to help out the creatives and the developers who wouldn't have time to do certain things because they have to do other jobs to sustain themselves and their families. The Metaverse platform provides these people opportunities to earn money without having to worry about anything, including your welfare, housing, food, insurance, and all these things. They will be taken care of by the company itself.

Many business models are already set up to offer opportunities for people who want to create and share their ideas. The Metaverse platform is the official place where you find these opportunities. You will register here as a user and start sharing your content or gaming content. Your business model will be presented in front of all individuals who would like to use your service. There are a lot of other participants who have entered the metaverse platform, including programmers, developers, sellers, etc

These people have created their businesses to earn money from their services by offering them for sale. They are using techniques and tools

to help them earn money out of their ideas, creations, and the way they play with the world around them.

Many different opportunities are available in The Metaverse if you want to start a business.

Examples of the business models in Metaverse.

1. Metaverse care franchise

If you have a hospital, clinic, or drug store in Metaverse, you can open a business of running and managing it. This can also apply to any other service-providing business in the market. People with such companies become care franchise owners, and they make money from their services and help others. In metaverse franchise systems, people can come to the same facility and receive help. Metaverse franchise owners get money from their providers' work, which can be reliable or even profitable.

2. Metaverse financial management

You are not just an entertainer anymore; you have become a financial expert with the skills that make you an asset to your community within Metaverse! You will create a system of financial transactions in Metaverse, control transactions with the digital currency on the blockchain system, and even view information from other blockchains like Bitcoin and Ethereum nodes.

3. VR games design service

You have a passion for virtual reality games and know how to create them! The Metaverse allows you to make your own VR game and earn
money from it. You can start your studio, become a game designer, and create a more exciting or creative game from scratch.

4. Virtual reality blockchains development service

If you are a blockchain developer, you have the opportunity to start a business in Metaverse by creating new blockchains that others can use in their virtual reality projects or on their websites, as well as developing new services and applications for Metaverse and other blockchains. You can also design your blockchain system and help others build applications while paying you for each development application.

5. Virtual phone assistant service

Many virtual assistants can manage your life in Metaverse. These AI-powered virtual assistants can manage your financial affairs, such as appointments or meetings, and automate task creation and completion. They can even power a Facebook chatbot in a way that makes them respond faster and more efficiently to customers' requests.

6. Virtual bodyguard service

Live in a Metaverse world where people have the option of hiring an escort, doctor, assistant, or therapist to their location. The job is to provide services for them and make it through their journey. You can also offer the same service for other people in your Metaverse world!

7. Virtual restaurants

If you are interested in creating a restaurant business in Metaverse, you can offer any food you want. For example, if you can create a delicious
burger for your customers, you will start a successful business. You can also make pizza using a 3D kitchen from your imagination.

8. Virtual retail store

If you have a passionate interest in fashion and design or are just a trendsetter who loves to dress others, then you can start your clothing or accessory store in Metaverse.

9. Remote services If you have an empty house or apartment with no one to live in it, the solution is to rent it out temporarily through the VR space of Metaverse! You can ask for rental prices for each month directly from the client's point of view; the longer their rental period is, the lower the rate will be.

10. Hire a team of people in Metaverse

One of the biggest challenges to entrepreneurs today is the need for a strong, committed, and reliable team of workers. But through Metaverse, you can create a virtual/digital/3D world that users can access from all over the world, which means you don't have to look for workers physically. If your business needs more workers, you can hire freelancers who are experts in their fields, who will work for you on-demand through Metaverse.

Business opportunities are so tremendous in Metaverse, and there are so many solutions for business owners and entrepreneurs out there. The only limitation is your imagination! Metaverse aspires to build a more sustainable economy in which the worth of digital assets may be
quantified and transferred layer by layer. The initial phase involves building an environment where people may trade digital assets using Metaverse's digital currency and identities. The next step is creating The Metaverse blockchain system, which will support applications in some specific areas such as game design, digital financial management, VR bodyguard services, etc.

# Conclusion

In conclusion, The Metaverse is just a virtual space where we can all exist on the internet. The Metaverse is a massive hub where we can share our dreams, thoughts, and even reality with other users in the world. We need to be aware of this digital space's vast power over us and use it wisely to make ourselves happy. It would also be wise to create our reality online, so we don't get lost in what others think they know about us. Creating your reality will ensure that these realities will not dictate your happiness or how you live your life.

The Metaverse will bring a new level of interaction and entertainment to the world. Its forces have been gathering for many years, awaiting a chance to come out in front to control us all. We must remain vigilant over our true identities and actions.

This world will bring a new sense of individualism and collectiveness. A world in which we can build upon our thoughts and dreams about our reality, using the available resources on the internet. A world in which we can be who we want to be and interact with other people in new ways from what is often perceived as real life. This Metaverse may include virtual worlds like Second Life and Everquest with interactions that mirror the natural world without many fundamental world limitations.

Metaverse is broad and can be defined as many things. Some people describe it as The Metaverse itself, while others describe it as the online aspect of our lives. In a way, they are the same. The Metaverse is our existence within this virtual space and is the space where our dreams, thoughts, and creations exist.

Metaverse applies in many aspects of our lives, not just in the online world. We all know that we have to be careful about what others think of us when making plans. Not everyone will like the same things we do, and we need to realize that if our actions don't reflect others' feelings about us, why should they be accurate? If a person doesn't like our appearance, does it make us real? If someone thinks we act differently than others do, is it true?

They are always thinking about these things within this world and never honestly know what others feel. With Metaverse, however, societies can interact more deeply than ever before. They can interact with others and give each other a chance to find out what they are like. They can meet in this virtual space, who may even become friends with people they have never met in the real world. Metaverse is a place to get together and meet people and share your thoughts, dreams, and ideas. We should use it as an outlet for our creativity to avoid wasting our time away from this virtual space.

If we genuinely want to be creative in this virtual space, why would we need to go back into the real world? We should use it to our fullest potential. In the virtual world, everything is achievable. Hence, we should try and utilize our full potential.

If we are meant to be creative within this space, why not give it a chance? Why shouldn't we create something truly incredible as a person in this virtual space? We are all given the ability to do so, and we should use it wisely. There is no reason to be afraid of being creative or making something new out of your designs.

Metaverse is applied in; films, books, games, and much more. It is the virtual space of our minds and can meet others who share similar interests to us. A metaverse is a place where your thoughts are alive, and you can interact with them in many ways. It is the place where you can be yourself in a new way that most people understand. It is the contemporary way societies come together as one virtual society that reflects themselves within their natural world counterpart.

The future of Metaverse is limitless. It can be used to create art, writing, music, and more. But everything it does will be for a better place for humans to live in the world. We are selfish beings and need this virtual space as an outlet for our creativity to make everything we do genuinely incredible from both our thoughts and actions. We need this to flourish so that we can grow as creative beings.